Deep Discipleship for Dark Days

A Manual for Holding Fast to What Is Good

Paul Dirks

ISBN: 978-1-989169-28-5

Deep Discipleship for Dark Days is an essential book for the body of Christ during these unprecedented times. Faithful to God's Word while applying it to the world around us, it will serve as a powerful tool for Christians trying to make sense of what is going on. I recommend it wholeheartedly.

- Alex Newman, Journalist, Evangelist, & Author

Paul Dirks is a thoughtful writer and faithful pastor. Both of the title phrases in his *Deep Discipleship for Dark Days* are astutely chosen. We live in a dark and difficult period in Western history, and Paul addresses these current challenges in a relevant and timely way, standing firmly on scriptural principles. He has provided us in this volume a valuable book on whole-life discipleship containing a clear call to action to protect, encourage and build for the Kingdom of God at personal, familial, and community levels. A positive contribution to the literature on discipleship.

- Rev. Dr. Joseph Boot, Founder & President of the Ezra Institute

Paul Dirks' book helps expose the seismic shifts taking place in our increasingly antichrist culture, while providing the reader with hope-filled and tangible responses to the darkness of our age. If you are looking for wise insight into our times, to galvanize yourself and your family from its lies, and to reshape the culture, I commend this fine work to you.

- Dr. Aaron Rock, Lead Pastor, Harvest Bible Church, Windsor

While it's tempting to become disheartened, even despondent, by the advancing secular onslaught undermining religious freedoms, assaulting Christian values, and threatening Christian witness, this is not our calling as followers of Christ. In his timely and accessible work, *Deep Discipleship for Dark Days*, Paul Dirks details what a faithful response looks like. His insightful read of the times juxtaposed with grounding Scripture sets the necessary backdrop for a call to perseverance of the saints through intentional discipleship efforts. This survival strategy for the soul outlines ways to think Christianly about contemporary challenges and provides practical direction for meaningful cultural engagement. Rather than a doom and gloom despairing, Paul Dirks encourages a hopeful desiring for gospel favour, as we keep our eyes on Jesus, the Author and Perfector of our faith.

- Dr. Ted Fenske, Clinical Professor with the Division of Cardiology at the University of Alberta, & Elder at Fellowship Baptist Church, Edmonton

DEDICATION

To my children, who may have to grow up in a world very different than the one in which I was raised: trials and tribulation are sure to come, and particularly for the godly. No matter the future, God has given you everything necessary for a life of godliness and productivity so that you may attain glory at Christ's return. Be faithful, and you will have the crown.

ACKNOWLEDGMENTS

Thank you to the Elders and members of New West Community Church for a break from regular preaching duties in order to write this book. May it produce maturity and readiness, and not only for our own sakes, but for those around us as well.

Contents

Introduction

EVERYTHING CAN CHANGE IN A MOMENT

"There are decades where nothing happens; and there are weeks where decades happen." This quote, often attributed to Vladimir Lenin, first head of the USSR, has murky origins. Among the possible geneses is his statement, "But in a revolution, the masses are in motion; the developments of years are compressed into months and days." Lenin had first-hand experience of this in the Bolshevik Revolution of 1917, but one does not have to look very hard to find further examples of this principle in history. We may lament some of these sudden changes, like the rise of Communism in Russia or the French Revolution, but positive developments, such as the tearing down of the Berlin Wall, can often take place just as suddenly.

Political upheavals are just one example of the sort of pivotal transformation which can occur very quickly. Natural disasters such as earthquakes, droughts, and infestations, are another example. From 1873 to 1876, enormous hordes of Rocky Mountain locusts, as many as 10 billion in a single swarm, destroyed crops throughout the plains and midwest of the United States.[1] The devastation of farmland led to abject poverty among many families, and it was an incredible miracle when the swarming plagues mysteriously disappeared, never to plague North America again.[2] This somewhat modern scourge calls to mind

---

[1]   Douglas Main, "Why Insect Populations Are Plummeting–And Why It Matters," *National Geographic*, February 2, 2019, www.nationalgeographic.com/animals/article/why-insect-populations-are-plummeting-and-why-it-matters.

[2]   Although secular historians and biologists have their theories to explain the extinction of the Rocky Mountain Locust, the true story may be the power of prayer.

the biblical plagues upon Egypt which resulted in cataclysmic consequences for one of the greatest empires of the ancient world. It also
changed the course of history for Israel, with the Exodus being one of
the most foundational events in Scripture.

Although we have, in recent times, learned to mitigate the
worst outcomes of natural disasters,[3] there remains the very real possibility of cataclysm. Where I live, in the Greater Vancouver area of BC,
Canada, we are apparently overdue for a severe earthquake. Only a
decade ago a large earthquake to the east of Japan resulted in a tsunami
that flooded the Fukushima Nuclear Power Plant in the Tohoku region
of Honshu, Japan, leading to the second-worst nuclear disaster in history, after Chernobyl. Although it is a highly debatable point whether or
not there have been more natural disasters recently, a single event can
change everything in an instant. Yellowstone Park, for instance, sits
upon a large volcano which is largely responsible for its unique ecosys-
tem. Projections indicate that if this volcano ever erupted, it would kill
millions and devastate much of North America.[4]

Technological advancements over the last twenty years have
also brought about seismic changes. There is more processing power
in many people's wristwatches or Roomba robot vacuums than in the
most advanced university computers a couple of decades ago. And
the pace of change is likely to increase. Klaus Schwab, founder of the
World Economic Forum, wrote in 2016 of what he terms *The Fourth
Industrial Revolution*: "Contrary to the previous industrial revolutions,
this one is evolving at an exponential rather than linear pace. This is
the result of the multifaceted, deeply interconnected world we live in
and the fact that new technology begets newer and even more capable

---

The people of the state of Minnesota persuaded the new governor, John S. Pillsbury,
one of the founders of the Pillsbury company, to declare a day of prayer on April 26,
1877. The day started very warm, causing the locust eggs to hatch, but that night a
cold front moved in, eventually resulting in a blizzard, which killed the newly hatched
insects. See "The Great Minnesota Grasshopper Miracle," *Kinship Christian Radio*,
2014, https://kinshipradio.org/home/2014/08/07/the-great-minnesota-grasshopper-mir-
acle/.

3   Michael Shellenberger, *Apocalypse Never* (New York: HarperCollins, 2020),
4.

4   Victoria Jaggard, "Yellowstone Supervolcano May Rumble to Life Faster
Than," *National Geographic*, October 12, 2017, www.nationalgeographic.com/science/
article/yellowstone-supervolcano-erupt-faster-thought-science.

technology."[5] The mapping of the human genome, the advent of quantum computing, the proliferation and progress of artificial intelligence (AI), and scientific discoveries about human life which would have been considered science-fiction mere decades ago,[6] are just a few of the enormous and fast-moving changes to our world. Economics and information access have been greatly impacted by the ubiquitous use of the Internet and the devices connected to it. A few multi-billion-dollar technology platforms control, at least to some degree, much of which goods we buy, what news we read, what friends we make, and perhaps even how we vote.[7]

In the sphere of health, the spread of COVID-19 and the resultant response by world governments and health organizations has been an event (or perhaps a series of cascading events) that many believe will change human society and history ever after. Many world leaders have in fact signalled that this is an opportunity to significantly remake our world, many of them using the same slogan—"Build Back Better"[8]—and several openly adhering to the World Economic Forum's plan for a "Great Reset."[9] Whether or not you believe that there are unanswered questions regarding everything that has taken place during

---

5   Klaus Schwab, *The Fourth Industrial Revolution* (New York: Crown Business, 2017), 3.

6   One example is the field of epigenetics and the discovery that behaviour can change the expression of one's genome, and those genomic changes can be passed down throughout multiple generations. See Tim Spector, *Identically Different: Why We Can Change Our Genes* (New York: The Overlook Press, 2014).

7   On the significant and biased role Facebook and Mark Zuckerberg played in the 2020 U.S. election, see Mollie Hemingway, *Rigged* (Washington, DC: Regnery Publishing, 2021), 191–223.

8   "To Build Back Better, We Must Reinvent Capitalism. Here's How," *World Economic Forum*, July 13, 2020, https://www.weforum.org/agenda/2020/07/to-build-back-better-we-must-reinvent-capitalism-heres-how/. The "Build Back Better" slogan, clearly attached to the World Economic Forum's current Great Reset initiative, has been used in connection with environmentally-sensitive disaster recovery initiatives sponsored by the United Nations (UN) for many years.

9   "Prime Minister Trudeau Speaks with His Royal Highness The Prince of Wales and the Commonwealth Group of Permanent Representatives to the United Nations," *Prime Minister of Canada, Government of Canada*, June 11, 2020, https://pm.gc.ca/en/news/readouts/2020/06/11/prime-minister-trudeau-speaks-his-royal-highness-prince-wales-and. "Today, The Prince of Wales' Sustainable Markets Initiative, in partnership with the World Economic Forum launched a major global initiative, #TheGreatReset. The Great Reset aims to reset, reimagine, rebuild, redesign, reinvigorate and rebalance our world in the wake of the COVID-19 pandemic." *The Royal Family*, "#TheGreatReset," *YouTube*, 2020, https://www.youtube.com/watch?v=hRPQqfwwuhU.

the COVID pandemic, we can all agree that it came upon the general public unexpectedly. And the world may never again be the same.

READY, SET, APOCALYPSE

Whether rapid societal changes come from the political, natural, technological, or biological spheres, these historical occurrences urge us to live in such a way that we are ready with a faithful response. In the gospels, Jesus clearly warned His followers to be prepared: "Be on guard, keep awake. For you do not know when the time will come" (Mk 13:33). The apostle Paul likewise alerted the faithful, "While people are saying, 'There is peace and security,' then sudden destruction will come upon them as labor pains come upon a pregnant woman, and they will not escape. But you are not in darkness, brothers, for that day to surprise you like a thief'" (1 Thes 5:3–4). These and other scriptural warnings do not necessarily refer to the same events. Sometimes the destruction of Jerusalem in AD 70 is in view, sometimes it is the return of Jesus Christ at the end of the age, and in some passages both ideas seem woven together and may be difficult to parse. Nevertheless, they impress upon the mind two basic principles.

The first is that we are to live in constant readiness for whatever may come, whether it be blessing or suffering, wealth or poverty, life or death. This is the basic, but radical discipleship of the scriptures. In addition to this general readiness, however, there are times in which particular signs of coming upheaval and tribulation are to be discerned. For instance, Jesus castigated the crowds in Luke 12:54–56,

> When you see a cloud rising in the west, you say at once, "A shower is coming." And so it happens. And when you see the south wind blowing, you say, "There will be scorching heat," and it happens. You hypocrites! You know how to interpret the appearance of earth and sky, but why do you not know how to interpret the present time?

These two axioms—a constant, general preparedness, and a particular discerning of the times (1 Chr 12:32) —are interconnected. In times of cataclysm, general readiness is rarely overturned, but it is rendered even more important. For instance, we are always to live without much investment in the things of this world (Mt 6:19–20). However, this principle becomes particularly important when the believer needs to escape God's judgment upon the city, leaving everything behind (Lk 17:31–32). The specific warnings may require a new course of action—leaving your cloak behind, for instance—but they are consistent with the normative but radical call to hold the things of this world lightly.

This book aims to address the first, more general principle, in light of the second, more specific one. I want to prepare you for a coming cataclysm in which evil powers and principalities will unite in a singular purpose; in which pressure, pleasure, and persecution will bring the masses into subjection, and in which widespread economic and societal upheaval will erode long-established traditions and structures. Even now, there are signs of this apocalyptic trajectory, some of which are clearly disclosed in the book of Revelation. The word "apocalypse," in fact, means "revelation," although I will use it throughout this book in its popular usage to refer to tumult or tribulation associated with end-of-the-world type patterns.

These patterns, it is worth noting, may not necessarily signal the final return of Christ. At times in the past, as recently as World War II, which will be referenced frequently in this book, many of these same patterns were seen and reached a point of climax. Yet God granted the grace of more time for repentance (2 Pt 3:9). One day, however, the Lord Jesus will return bodily and usher in the fullness of His reign. I do not know when that day will come, and this book makes no chronological predictions of His return. It may be two years, twenty years, or even two hundred years away. But we must always live ready.

Whether or not the current trajectory culminates in Christ's return soon or not, you will need a survival strategy for your soul, a battle-plan in order to be a conqueror in the coming cataclysm. This book will at times call for a specific course of action in connection with particular apocalyptic-flavoured events, but for the most part it enjoins the importance of a deep discipleship for these dark days.

FORTUNE-TELLING

Apocalyptic warnings are nothing new. A strong argument could be made that almost every generation has had voices proclaiming the end of the world. Whether these voices belonged to educated futurologists pointing to the implications of the latest advances, or charismatic prophets claiming to be the mouthpieces of God, these proclamations have rarely been lacking. In addition, and disconcertingly, many of these prophets have profited, at least temporarily, from their visions.

In Max Dublin's *Future Hype*, he recounts the story of Bedward, a Jamaican prophet in the 1920s who predicted "the end of white rule and his direct ascent with his followers to heaven."[10] His message caught fire, fueled by the recent cataclysms of World War I and a local earthquake. Thousands followed him, selling their belongings and even their land in order to fly away with him. The prophesied rapture did not occur. And as is often the case, it was the poorest who suffered the greatest loss by listening to the charismatic charlatan. Modern Christian evangelicalism has fared little better. Hal Lindsey's *The Late Great Planet Earth* was the best-selling nonfiction book of the 1970s. It has been translated into more than fifty languages and not only did it sell 28 million copies by 1990, it also sold another 7 million the next decade in spite of its failed prophecies![11] When faced with these and other examples, it almost appears as if the masses want to be duped. Or perhaps the sins of fortune-telling are more deeply embedded than we think, preying, as they do, upon the imprinted human hope in an eternal paradise.

I have not been immune to this kind of thinking. I remember reading a fascinating book in my early teens about Saddam Hussein and how he would usher in the end times predicted in Revelation.[12]

---

10   Max Dublin, *Futurehype: The Tyranny of Prophecy* (Markham, ON: Penguin Books Canada, 2989), 7–9.

11   Erin A. Smith, "The Late Great Planet Earth Made the Apocalypse a Popular Concern," *Humanities* 38, no. 1 (2017), https://www.neh.gov/humanities/2017/winter/feature/the-late-great-planet-earth-made-the-apocalypse-popular-concern.

12   The book was Charles Dyer's *The Rise of Babylon: Sign of the End Times* (Wheaton, IL: Tyndale House Publishers, 1991).

There was a certain adrenalin-fueled appeal to piecing together the puzzle and undercurrents of contemporary crises and finding a Bible passage (or even the remotest inference from one) which seemed to fit the recent situation perfectly. It is an understandable human mechanism. And it is so often wrong.

Prophets of doom, however, do not arise in the religious sphere alone. Man is a religious creature and even atheists cannot resist the temptation to prophesy. In the late '60s, Paul Ehrlich wrote in *The Population Bomb*, that "the battle to feed all humanity is over. In the 1970s and 1980s hundreds of millions of people will starve to death in spite of any crash programs embarked upon now."[13] More recently, apocalyptic scenarios have emerged around climate change. In a recent opinion-editorial in *The New York Post*, author-researcher Bjørn Lomborg reviewed just a few of the failed doomsday scenarios of the peddlers of the climate crisis.[14] In 1972, the organizer of the first UN environmental summit warned that we had "just 10 years to avoid catastrophe."[15] Ten years later, in 1982, the UN predicted that by the year 2000 there would be "devastation as complete, as irreversible as any nuclear holocaust."[16] This is the kind of "exaggeration, alarmism, and extremism" that caused Michael Shellenberger to write *Apocalypse Never*, which demonstrates, using the best-available science, the hypocrisies, inconsistencies, and irrational thinking underpinning much of modern environmentalism's doomsday message.[17]

Although at the time of writing we are still in the process of separating fact from fiction, it seems inescapable that apocalyptic scenarios have also played a significant role in the world's response to the emergence of COVID. The modelling and predictions by now-disgraced UK mathematical epidemiologist Neil Ferguson were largely

---

13   Shellenberger, *Apocalypse Never*, 237.

14   Bjorn Lomborg, "The Comic Cries of Climate Apocalypse — 50 Years of Spurious Scaremongering," *New York Post*, November 30, 2021, https://nypost.com/2021/11/30/the-comic-cries-of-climate-apocalypse-50-years-of-spurious-scaremongering/.

15   Lomborg, "The Comic Cries."

16   Lomborg "The Comic Cries."

17   Shellenberger, *Apocalypse Never*, xiii.

responsible for severe world-wide lockdowns.[18] He predicted that 2.2 million Americans and more than 500,000 in the UK could die from COVID as ICU capacity was overwhelmed. In New York, the USNS Comfort hospital ship was purposed to accept an overflow that never came as the ship remained mostly empty.[19] Texas' end to their mask mandate in early March of 2021 is another example. The Governor's decision was decried by NIAID president Dr. Anthony Fauci as "really quite risky," and President Joe Biden stated that the Texas Republican leaders were engaged in "Neanderthal thinking."[20] A month later Dr. Fauci was at a loss to explain why cases had not risen in the Lone Star State.[21]

These events could merely be examples of the experts knowing far less than they are often given credit for—they are simply poor prophets like the rest of us.[22] The more alarming possibility is that there are other purposes behind the predictions. Whether or not these modern apocalypticists in environmentalism or medicine are knowingly harnessing the hidden power of prophecy, it has always been the case that, as Max Dublin states, "Predictions have power: there is no rhetorical or propaganda device more powerful than prophecy. Predictions do not simply describe the world—they *act* on it."[23] Although it was given in a different context, we may do well to apply the Old Testament test of prophecy to these modern doomsday predictors: "When a prophet speaks in the name of the LORD, if the word does not come to pass

---

18   John Fund, "'Professor Lockdown' Modeler Resigns in Disgrace," *The National Review*, May 6, 2020, https://www.nationalreview.com/corner/professor-lock-down-modeler-resigns-in-disgrace/.

19   Ashley Collman, "How USNS Comfort Went from a Symbol of Hope with the President's Blessing, to Heading Back from NYC Having Treated Fewer than 180 Patients," *Business Insider*, April 26, 2020, https://www.businessinsider.com/usns-comfort-nyc-coronavirus-timeline-2020-4.

20   Carlie Porterfield, "Dr. Fauci: Texas And Mississippi Mask Mandate Rollbacks Are 'Ill-Advised' And 'Risky,'" *Forbes*, March 3, 2021, https://www.forbes.com/sites/carlieporterfield/2021/03/03/dr-fauci-texas-and-mississippi-mask-mandate-rollbacks-are-ill-advised-and-risky/?sh=10736bdc1611.

21   Kathianne Boniello, "Fauci 'Not Sure' Why Texas Doesn't Have COVID Uptick after Nixing Masks," *New York Post*, April 10, 2021, https://nypost.com/2021/04/10/fauci-not-sure-why-texas-doesnt-have-covid-uptick-after-nixing-masks/.

22   For more on the dangerous role of "experts" in our current culture, see chapter 3.

23   Dublin, *Futurehype*, 5.

or come true, that is a word that the LORD has not spoken; the prophet has spoken it presumptuously. You need not be afraid of him" (Dt 18:22).

LIVING READY

I bring up these examples to raise a question that could be leveled at this book—that I am fearmongering in order to drag people back in line with religious sentiments and traditional values, which benefits Christianity and the church. Ultimately, the reader will have to decide for himself, but my initial response to this is quite simple. As already mentioned, when it comes to the general principles that undergird most of the book, these are simply the normative, albeit radical, truths of living according to Christ's commands. In those places where I do engage in prognostication, I have kept to facts that are readily available and demonstrable.

I will mention two examples. Short of a worldwide revolution or revival, there is a biometrically linked digital identification coming. It may start at the national level, but it will become global. When I deal with this further in chapter five, I will demonstrate that significant numbers of co-ordinated non-profits, tech giants, nations, and multi-billionaires are working openly and publicly on this project. It is not remotely hidden. It is couched in moral idioms and hailed as justice and equality, but it does not take much investigation to discover.

Another example is the digital surveillance of almost every aspect of our lives and behaviour, a growing technological omniscience that Shoshana Zuboff, riffing off of Orwell's *1984,* calls "Big Other" in her meticulously researched *The Age of Surveillance Capitalism.*[24] Whether or not these data extraction and behavioural modification systems will ever be controlled by a global elite or a "man of lawlessness" in our lifetimes is speculative; that these artificial intelligence systems are operative right now and constitute a financially fueled locomotive which would require a miracle to slow or stop, is a fact.

---

24 Shoshana Zuboff, *The Age of Surveillance Capitalism* (New York: PublicAffairs, 2019), 376.

These and other emerging forces are beginning to threaten our faith and integrity in ways that most of us, at least in the West, have never encountered. This unknown ought not to cause anxiety or fear for the Christian, however. We may not know fully what is coming or what it will look like when it does, but the seven principles of this book will work nonetheless, grounded as they are in realities which surpass what we see with our eyes. This is the only safe way to proceed, for we always look as through a glass darkly (1 Cor 13:12). These exhortations build from the more general to the more specific, and to some degree from the more personal to the more global.

Firstly, you must be ready to fight for what is important in this world. We live in a world of a false and manufactured "peace" by which dark powers are gaining ascendancy. The battle is not against flesh and blood, but it does manifest itself in the world, and you will need to engage in this warfare not with bullets or steel, but with words—words of truth. As Jesus states at a very particular point in history, if you do not own a sword, "buy one" (Lk 22:36).

The second exhortation is to "flee the carnival," that is to stop living your life pursuing ease and entertainment. The wealth to which we have become so accustomed in the West is likely to be our undoing. Subtle addictions will compromise the integrity of many as they are slowly boiled like a frog in the proverbial pot, unwilling and unable to escape the world and its coming judgment.[25]

Thirdly, "resist the mind-control" in order to escape the powers of persuasion that infect our world. We are living in a dumbed-down age in which we are spoon-fed prepared narratives and led astray by pagan ideologies. Increasingly uncommon are true thinkers who read books, evaluate ideas, and reflect on their implications. For better or for worse, our minds are plastic and they need discipline and renewal to discern the times and respond accordingly.

The fourth chapter concerns the deliberate destruction of the

---

25   God created the world good, and Christ's lordship restores the created order, including the world as man's habitation. We must not too greatly dichotomize the material and the spiritual. At times, however, the Scriptures use the word "world" to designate fallen and rebellious creation in hostility to Christ and His people (Jn 15:19, Jas 4:4, 1 Jn 2:16).

family—the foundation of human society. The forces arrayed against parents and their children are as subtle as they are strong and much "home-work" will be needed to preserve the most important institution in the world and leave a heritage as God intends. In light of the hostility of the world, our homes should not only be havens, they should also be headquarters.

Chapter five begins to look further outward. Many, if not most, of our traditional institutions are severely compromised by cowardice and worldly ideologies, including Christian ones. They are rotting from the inside out, and we will need to build new structures to withstand the pressures of these evil days, especially if social ostracization begins. A new frontier is opening up and we need to "practice pioneering."

The penultimate chapter attempts to unmask some of the abominations associated with world-influencing powers which are currently gaining a greater foothold in culture. In light of these evils, there is an ethical imperative which cannot come at too high a cost. We will need to be ready to draw strong lines, and even to give up our lives, rather than be implicated in these horrendous evils—we must not "dine with demons."

The last exhortation is to "find the faithful." There is tremendous ethical compromise in the evangelical church, and the dedicated disciple will need to find assemblies which apply the gospel to all of life, whose leaders are ready to suffer for the faith, and who will support you in the spiritual struggle as brothers-in-arms.

TRUTH AND TRIBULATION

This book is informed by two main areas of personal experience—pastoring and political advocacy. I have had the privilege of pastoring and preaching for twenty years in different roles. The call of the preacher is to seek out the meaning inherent in God's Word, and then to exhort the world, and especially the faithful, to believe and obey it. Early on in my ministry I noted an uncomfortable but necessary truth, namely that the scriptural example of prophecy and preaching evidences a second-person imperative style. The one speaking for God is to put himself in the place of God and address himself to the "you" of his audience, making demands of them as those under obligation to God. In this way, the activity of the pulpit stands starkly apart from the advice and self-help material of the world.

In contrast to this scriptural model, it is common for modern preachers to use the proverbial "we" in an effort to place themselves, humbly it is thought, within the mass of those needing the same message. Although there is a nugget of truth to this modern approach, it nevertheless undermines the basic essence of preaching—the prophetic. As I have done my best over the years to speak as one speaking the very oracles of God (1 Pt 4:11), I have had to wrestle week by week with what I plan to definitively proclaim. This is a necessary but highly discomforting process! The results, it seems to me, can only be one of two things: hypocritical Pharisaism or a weekly and painful submission to Scripture's difficult demands—a sort of death, if you will. In this process, however, the one proclaiming truth is both transformed and forced to overcome his natural cowardice to speak what is uncomfortable.

Although perhaps not as a matter of course, this kind of prophetic speech leads to marketplace-speaking and, in my personal experience, political advocacy on issues of sexual orientation and gender identity (SOGI), especially as they relate to women's sex-based rights and the protection of children. The public preaching of God's Word, and the preparation that precedes it, is one kind of refining fire. Political advocacy on forbidden topics is another.

Over the last several years, I have spoken to the Senate on Canada's now-infamous Bill C-16,[26] been one of the key leaders of the *One Accord*,[27] organized public protests, and trained hundreds of

---

26   Bill C-16 added gender identity and gender expression to the Canadian Human Rights Act, and was passed on June 15, 2017 in the Senate. "Bill C-16, An Act to Amend the Canadian Human Rights Act and the Criminal Code : Wednesday, May 10, 2017" (Senate of Canada, 2017), https://sencanada.ca/en/committees/LCJC/noticeof-meeting/452675/42-1.

27   The *One Accord*, originally called *The West Coast Christian Accord*, is a Canadian statement on Scripture's teaching on sexuality and gender, signed at the time of its unveiling on September 26, 2018 by two hundred pastors across Canada.

church leaders in Canada on sex and gender issues. But I have also been compared to a neo-Nazi by regional news, had our church protested by gender-activists, and had a multi-church all-candidates meeting canceled by our local Member of Parliament, publicly naming me as hateful and bigoted. To state the obvious, these latter circumstances are not enjoyable or desirable. But they are helpful in knowing how our world thinks, where the battle is, and the price each one must pay to maintain his faith and integrity.

I will be drawing from my experience in the fields of both pastoral ministry and political advocacy in the book's seven main exhortations. Although I have endeavoured to demonstrate the wisdom of these principles from a variety of sources both spiritual and secular, the truths contained in Scripture are crucial to this book's thesis, and thus it must be a predominantly spiritual book. Only the truth of God's word provides an overarching narrative that explains what will come, why it is permitted, the good that will come of it, and how everything is linked together. Secular sources can be useful in bringing to light certain aspects of crisis or cataclysm, but they are unable to connect it to the broader picture we see in the Bible. Moreover, it is through the scriptures alone that we can unveil the spiritual side of the apocalypse. The secularist may indeed see that there is a "devil" behind certain events (an idiom I have heard many times from unbelievers), but it is only through the Spirit of Christ that anyone is able to ascertain Satan's true motives or strategies. As the apostle Paul says, "we are not ignorant of his designs" (2 Cor 2:11).

Lastly, only the gospel of Jesus Christ is able to offer true hope in times of tribulation. Although I make no predictions of the timing of apocalyptic scenarios or Christ's return, the scriptures are clear that there will be a time prior to the end—whether soon, or yet still many years away—in which dark powers will be given free reign and dominion for a short while (Dn 7:21, Rv 13:7). At that time the "fight" against dark powers will not have *earthly* success. The fight

Rachel Browne, "How a Proposed Conversion Therapy Ban and LGBTQ2 Issues Are Mobilizing Canada's Christian Right," *Global News*, July 22, 2019, https://globalnews.ca/news/5511047/conversion-therapy-ban-3/.

will still honor Christ and result in glories which the faithful will share with Him at His return, but the secularist will at that time have no hope, because he has no belief beyond the material. Even at present, however, the gospel and the words of Jesus offer the only true hope, joy, and peace that is able to keep us steadfast and unshakeable though surrounded by evils: "I will not be afraid of many thousands of people who have set themselves against me all around" (Ps 3:6).

Although the principles in this book are useful for all believers, I have written with two main groups in mind. Firstly, I am concerned for those who are theologically minded and have a track record of faithfulness, yet seem oblivious to the dangers that are rising around them and the rapid changes which threaten their integrity, fruitfulness, or even their souls. As we will see, some of the growing pressures of our world-system are subtle. Because of the relative comfort of their lives, many of these people are not ready for the tribulation that may come at any time. They assume they are living in peacetimes and are late to the game in drawing battlelines. Meanwhile, the Beast-system is deploying its propaganda, spies, and guerillas, readying for all-out warfare. My hope is that this book serves as a warning to this well-meaning, but unprepared group.

I am also concerned, however, about those who see some of the potentially seismic changes occurring at present and are fearful or depressed, easily overcome by the latest news, or consumed with unearthing the identity of the world's supervillains in their internet-sleuthing. I know far too many people who are anxiety-laden because of these worries about the future. I do not doubt that some of their unearthed conspiracy-theories may be conspiracy-facts. It is beyond doubt, however, that any pursuit which has as its regular outcome anxiety, depression, or fear, is not the fruit of God's Spirit. The Christian ought to spend more time working against evil powers than discovering their secret identities; more time praying the promises of God's Word than trying to put the puzzle pieces together; more time sharing the gospel of salvation than sharing their recent findings on social media.

It is possible that this latter group may wish for more in this book—more specifics, more details, more prognostication. This is not my purpose, however. This book is not chiefly about vaccines, mandates, or big pharma. It is not primarily concerned with Bill Gates, George Soros, or Klaus Schwab. It is not ultimately about the World Economic Forum, the UN, or the Global Elite either. This book is about you. It is about surviving the coming cataclysm with your soul secured and your integrity intact. It is about having peace, joy, and purpose in the midst of tribulation. It is about fighting a good fight, keeping the faith, and winning a prize at the end of it all (2 Tm 4:7–8).

CHAPTER 1

Buy a Sword

EMBRACE THE ADVENTURE

James Chalmers was born in Scotland in 1841 and grew up in a fishing village where he was known for his aquatic adventures, narrowly escaping death by drowning on several occasions.[1] This adventurous spirit was turned towards the South Pacific when as an eighteen-year-old he was converted at an evangelistic meeting that he had attended only in order to cause trouble.[2] Chalmers was eventually called by God to brave the deep spiritual darkness of New Guinea. It was a work of constant danger; he was shipwrecked four times,[3] his life was regularly threatened by the indigenous cannibals, and the tropical diseases which menaced foreigners eventually claimed both his first and second wives.[4] But God used Chalmers' fiery enthusiasm, strong personality, and unshakable faith to transform New Guinea. Throughout his life, the Scotsman trained dozens of martyr-minded indigenous leaders, baptized hundreds of New Guineans, saw churches of thousands established, and effected widespread societal change.[5] Having spent several weeks on shipboard with Chalmers on one occasion, the great novelist Robert Louis Stevenson, author of *Treasure Island* and other adventure tales, wrote of the great missionary, "He took me fairly by storm

---

1   Eugene Myers Harrison, "James Chalmers: The Greatheart Of New Guinea," in *Giants of the Missionary Trail* (Chicago: Scripture Press Foundation, 1954), 131, https://archive.org/details/giantsofmissiona00harr.

2   Harrison, "James Chalmers," 132.

3   Harrison, "James Chalmers," 153.

4   Harrison, "James Chalmers," 142, 156.

5   Harrison, "James Chalmers," 145, 155–156.

for the most attractive, simple, brave and interesting man in the whole Pacific."[6]

I love missionary biographies. Throughout the years we have read many of them around the dinner table or during summer vacation. One of the things I appreciate about them is how they fittingly uphold the courage, strength, and hope of man in the midst of a great struggle—sometimes to overcome persecution and evil powers, and sometimes simply to survive. Life is struggle. Jesus Christ said, "in this world you will have tribulation" (Jn 16:33). Portraying the same truth more optimistically, however, we might say that life is an adventure.

The success of first-person shooter video games, the popularity of American football, and the box office returns of Marvel superhero movies suggest that we have not completely lost our martial instinct as a race. When it comes to the real world, however, adventure is more desired than experienced and many roll over when the first real threat raises its head. At the risk of bias, I will venture that this is nowhere more apparent than in Canada, my home country. Canadians are peace-lovers and peacemakers. We are known for being the friendly folks with maple leaf flags on our backpacks as we travel the world, making friends, and needlessly apologizing. We would be happy to live by Jesus' dictum of non-resistance, "if anyone slaps you on the right cheek, turn to him the other also," (Mt 5:39) but some of Christ's other words appear to us somewhat more foreign:

> I came to cast fire on the earth, and would that it were already kindled! I have a baptism to be baptized with, and how great is my distress until it is accomplished! Do you think that I have come to give peace on earth? No, I tell you, but rather division. (Lk 12:49–51)

> From the days of John the Baptist until now the kingdom of heaven has suffered violence, and the violent take it by force." (Mt 11:12)

In Luke 22, Jesus is only hours away from His final tribulation. His "baptism" is at hand, and ironically, through the suffering of death, He is himself about to lay siege to the gates of heaven on behalf of man.

---

6   Harrison, "James Chalmers," 144.

Three times previously in the book of Luke, Jesus spoke about the equipment of the true disciple (or the lack thereof). To the Twelve he stated, "Take nothing for your journey, no staff, nor bag, nor bread, nor money; and do not have two tunics." (Lk 9:3) In Luke 10:4, to the expanded group of seventy-two, He commanded, "Carry no moneybag, no knapsack, no sandals, and greet no one on the road." (Lk 10:4) And then once again, in Luke 12:33, He reassured them saying, "Fear not, little flock, for it is your Father's good pleasure to give you the kingdom. Sell your possessions, and give to the needy. Provide yourselves with moneybags that do not grow old, with a treasure in the heavens that does not fail, where no thief approaches and no moth destroys" (Lk 12:32–33). In light of these repeated instructions, it is perhaps surprising that before His passion He seems to instruct His disciples quite differently.

> "When I sent you out with no moneybag or knapsack or sandals, did you lack anything?" They said, "Nothing." He said to them, "But now let the one who has a moneybag take it, and likewise a knapsack. *And let the one who has no sword sell his cloak and buy one.* For I tell you that this Scripture must be fulfilled in me: 'And he was numbered with the transgressors.' For what is written about me has its fulfillment." And they said, "Look, Lord, here are two swords." And he said to them, "It is enough." (Lk 22:35–38)

There is an important sense in which the earlier commands are not overturned with this latter statement. The true follower of Jesus must continue to live as if he possessed nothing, in complete dependence upon God's provision, not worrying about what he will eat or drink. In another sense, however, the circumstances called out for a new approach to the disciple's belongings. It was a time of upheaval, and they needed to be ready. They needed a sword. Not too many— this wasn't an armed rebellion (Mt 26:52). But enough to defend themselves. Similarly, there is an upheaval—and adventure—which is almost upon us. If you have not already done so, either because of ignorance or cowardice, it is high time you listened to Christ and, symbolically, bought a sword.

Slaying the Serpent

The idea of the life-or-death struggle against an evil foe runs throughout Scripture beginning all the way back in Genesis. Symbolic fore-
bodings were embedded even in the account of the original creation.
"The earth was without form and void, and darkness was over the face
of the deep. And the Spirit of God was hovering over the face of the
waters" (Gn 1:2). There was something there—maybe not chaos, but
perhaps the possibility of chaos—even from the beginning. It is as if
God was saying to Adam, "you were meant for a battle." This hint is
given structure in the dominion mandate later in the chapter. Man is
not only to "be"—made, as he is, in God's image, but to "do"—which
involves having dominion and subduing the earth (Gn 1:26–28). This
lordship and subjugation is to be comprehensive, taking in the spheres
of heavens, earth, and seas (Gn 1:28).[7] The human enterprise is to subdue all that is unstructured and wild through the order and implications
of God's law. This law was written upon man's heart. It was intrinsic to
him, imprinted upon his ethical faculties by his Creator.

After the Fall and the entrance of sin into the world, the unor-
dered turned into forces of chaos. The serpent became a great dragon
which threatened to devour him (Gn 4:7, 1 Pt 5:8). The beasts of the
world conspired to overturn the created order and subject him (Dt
32:34, Rv 13). The castle of hearth and home began to decay and fall
apart due to familial conflict (Gn 3:16). And man's struggle was no
longer merely with external forces willing to bow to tool and trade, but
increasingly with internal powers—the furnaces of his own desires and
the ensnaring appetites of his own flesh.

These themes are communicated in Scripture not only through
clear teaching, such as we find in the Epistles, but also through story
and "myth." I use the word "myth" cautiously, for I believe that even
the most symbolic and archetypal stories of Scripture are absolutely
true, Genesis 1 onward. But the idea of "myth"—a story shrouded in
symbolism using primeval characters and themes—is helpful because

---

7   Peter J. Leithart, *A House for My Name: A Survey of the Old Testament*
(Moscow, ID: Canon Press, 2000), 45.

it is memorable. These stories communicate effectively and capture the attention, even of children. Hence the scriptures, consistent with symbolism used in other Ancient Near-East writings, speak of chaos-monsters who are defeated and struck down by a champion in the heavens.[8]

> Awake, awake, put on strength, O arm of the LORD; awake, as in days of old, the generations of long ago. Was it not you who cut Rahab in pieces, who pierced the dragon? Was it not you who dried up the sea, the waters of the great deep, who made the depths of the sea a way for the redeemed to pass over? (Is 51:9–10)

> Let the heavens praise your wonders, O LORD, your faithfulness in the assembly of the holy ones! For who in the skies can be compared to the LORD? Who among the heavenly beings is like the LORD, a God greatly to be feared in the council of the holy ones, and awesome above all who are around him? O LORD God of hosts, who is mighty as you are, O LORD, with your faithfulness all around you? You rule the raging of the sea; when its waves rise, you still them. You crushed Rahab like a carcass; you scattered your enemies with your mighty arm. (Ps 89:5–10)

These monsters and beasts not only represented evil spiritual forces, they also represented nations and kings upon the earth. Egypt and Pharaoh, who so clearly opposed God's servant and His people in the book of Exodus, are called dragons (Ez 29:3, 32:2), and the four great kingdoms revealed to Daniel—Babylon, Persia, Greece, and Rome—were illustrated as beasts that came from the sea of chaos (Dn 7:3).[9] The book of Revelation picks up on the same theme when it describes Satan as a dragon thrown out of heaven that "became furious with the woman, and went off to make war on the rest of her offspring, on those who keep the commandments of God and hold to the testi-

---

8   Douglas Mangum and Matthew James Hamilton, "Leviathan," *Lexham Bible Dictionary* (Bellingham, WA: Lexham Press, 2016). The ANE sources are not necessary for understanding the biblical symbolism, and are themselves perversions of the fuller truths expressed in Scripture.

9   It ought to be noted that along with "chaos," the Gentile nations are also associated with the sea. Along these lines, the symbolism of the "beast-empire" is not wholly negative and James B. Jordan has argued that these beast-empires are to be tamed by "men" (Israel/Church) and that they are often given by God to protect God's people, as was the case in Joseph-Pharoah's Egypt, Daniel-Nebuchadnezzar's Babylon, and Esther-Darius' Persia. James B. Jordan, *The Handwriting on the Wall* (Powder Springs, GA: American Vision, 2007), 349–406.

mony of Jesus. And he stood on the sand of the sea" (Rv 12:17). It is from the sea that the Beast arises, answering to the Dragon's call, before another beast, the False Prophet, finally arises from the earth. The comprehensive triad of heavens, sea, and earth of Genesis 1 are replicated in the dominion that Satan wants to steal from mankind as God's representatives.

It is my experience that, for most people, meaning is communicated most effectively either by story or by proposition. For those in the second camp, let me make clear the meaning of these picture-texts: while our struggle is not *primarily* against flesh and blood (Eph 6:12), our struggle *will* spill out into the world of flesh and blood. As Francis Schaeffer states,

> The primary battle is a spiritual battle in the heavenlies. But this does not mean, therefore, that the battle we are in is otherworldly or outside of human history. It is a real spiritual battle, but it is equally a battle here on earth in our own country, our own communities, our places of work and our schools, and even our own homes. The spiritual battle has its counterpart in the visible world, in the minds of men and women, and in every area of human culture. In the realm of space and time the heavenly battle is fought on the stage of human history.[10]

This truth has implications not only for the life of faith but also for science, philosophy, and politics. Because man's sphere of dominion is to be comprehensive, our wielding of the "sword" is to be comprehensive too. It will not do for Christians to sign a peace treaty with the forces of evil. The Dragon, the Beast, and the False Prophet are vying for the same territory given to man and claimed by Christ, namely the entire world, and they are not afraid to use their "swords" or any other means to acquire it.

When the apostle Paul speaks of powers that are arrayed against God, he uses multiple words that likely connote both spiritual and physical authority. Colossians 1:16 states, "For by him all things were created, in heaven and on earth, visible and invisible, whether *thrones* or *dominions* or *rulers* or *authorities*—all things were created

---

10   Francis A. Schaeffer, *The Complete Works of Francis A. Schaeffer: A Christian Worldview*, vol. 4 (Westchester, IL: Crossway Books, 1982), 311–312.

through him and for him." Christ's dominion, as the second Adam, extends over all the earth and its various spheres. He is "the faithful witness, the firstborn of the dead, and the ruler of kings on earth" (Rv 1:5). Not only is the invisible "ruler of this world"—Satan—cast out of this world by heaven's king (Jn 12:31), but Christ reigns over literal flesh-and-blood rulers who are obligated to bow to Him and His law, and will one day do so even against their will (Phil 2:10–11). Those who claim Christ as Lord are left here as prophets, priests, and kings, in order to usher in His kingdom: "Thy kingdom come. Thy will be done on earth as it is done in heaven" (Mt 6:10). The question for us is how do we engage in this struggle? How do we use the sword not only against invisible spiritual forces, but also against subjugating heads of state, tyrannical technocrats, and iniquitous, influential entertainers who are visibly present in this world?

THE WEAPON OF THE WORD

Although it is possible that Jesus may be referring to a literal sword in Luke 22:36, and alluding to the necessity and propriety of defending one's life in times of physical danger, there are reasons to believe that Jesus may be speaking metaphorically of being "spiritually armed and prepared for battle against the spiritual foes," as Robert Stein theorizes.[11]

The symbolism of the sword in Scripture is closely connected with speech and its inherent power. Jesus, the Son of God, is called "the Word" (Jn 1:1). It is this Word, manifested in the world, that is both penetratingly painful (Lk 2:35, Heb 4:12) and deeply liberating (Jn 8:32). Those who receive Christ's implanted word are to now speak in the same way themselves. By a regenerating and animating word, the preeminent Word sends into the world a whole band of prophets who will do what He did and take up the sword of speaking God's truth.

The priority in this sword-speech is the good news of Jesus

---

11   Robert H. Stein, *Luke*, ed. New American Commentary (Nashville: Broadman & Holman Publishers, 1992), 555.

Christ which is able to save from sin and transform lives. But the gospel has implications. Firstly, the good news implies that we need to be saved from the terrible effects of our sins. Our message therefore needs to point out man's sinfulness against God and His judgment against us. This is unpopular to say the least, but it is the only thing that is going to save. I hear much talk today about revival and the love of God, but little about sin, judgment, and hell.[12] Francis Schaeffer made similar observations in his day.

> We are saying that we want reformation and we want revival, but still we are not preaching into this generation, stating the negative things that are necessary. If there is to be a constructive revolution in the orthodox, evangelical church, then like Jeremiah we must speak of the judgment of individual men great and small, of the church, the state, and the culture, for many of them have known the truth of God and have turned away from Him and His propositional revelation. God exists, He is holy, and we must know that there will be judgment. And like Jeremiah, we must keep on so speaking regardless of the cost to ourselves.[13]

True gospel preaching therefore requires courage and a sword. So does the dominion mandate. On one hand, we are to live quietly and work with our hands (1 Thes 4:11). We are to be "subject to the governing authorities" (Rom 13:1). We are to live in an honorable way even if outsiders view us as evil for the good we do (1 Pt 2:12). But this is a far cry from going along to get along in the world—Jesus died for what He said! Jesus' death was God's plan for man's salvation, but it was also the unjust execution of a man who threatened the power-structures and political leaders of His day. He lambasted the nation's rulers for their evils. He excoriated them for their self-serving interests. He refused to play their games or to allow them to entrap Him. When it came to protecting the most vulnerable—women, children, and foreigners—Christ had an even stronger approach! He was killed for it, and we should expect similar persecution, for a servant is not greater than his master. If they persecuted Christ as He exposed their sins, the

---

12 See Paul Dirks, *Is There Anything Good About Hell?* (New Westminster, BC: Decretum Books, 2021).

13 Schaeffer, *The Complete Works*, 255–256.

world will also persecute us when we expose theirs (Jn 15:20–22). This will be the reality for every person that takes up the sword of the Spirit—the Word of God (Eph 6:17).

In the book of Revelation, the symbol of Christ's Word as a sharp two-edged sword (Rv 1:16, 2:12) is later transformed into the image of two witnesses who pour fire out of their mouths and consume their foes (Rv 11:4). The imagery is multi-layered with the context calling to mind Moses and Elijah's feats against the "beasts" of their time.[14] These two legendary men of faith were endued with Spirit-power to perform miracles by mere words. In a similar way, their example encourages the church of Christ to keep speaking for Christ and against His enemies, knowing that not a hair on their heads will perish until the God-appointed time for their death (Lk 21:18). Even the word "two" has important connotations, communicating the idea of the unmitigated truth being declared, it being the minimum number of witnesses to establish truth in a court of law (Dt 19:15).

This symbolism is a reflection of the two divine speakers, the Son and the Spirit, who are sent by God the Father into the world to transform it. As the dark descends in the book of Revelation, this is why the Dragon also has two false witnesses—the Beast and the False Prophet.

> And the beast was captured, and with it the false prophet who in its presence had done the signs by which he deceived those who had received the mark of the beast and those who worshiped its image. These two were thrown alive into the lake of fire that burns with sulfur. And the rest were slain by the sword that came from the mouth of him who was sitting on the horse, and all the birds were gorged with their flesh. (Rv 19:20–21)

We will return to the Beast and its "mark" several times in this book. It is an important and much broader idea than many people generally assume. For now, we ought to observe that this evil, false god—the Dragon—sends two speakers to the earth. The Spirit and Son were

---

14   Pharoah and Ahab/Jezebel stand with Haman as clear anti-Christ figures in the Old Testament bent on eradicating the people of God.

sent by the Father to sacrifice and set free.[15] The Beast and the False Prophet are sent by the Dragon to set up a rebellious throne and subjugate. And if we care at all for the world, the glory of Christ, or justice, we must fight against these powers. We do this, like Moses, Elijah, and the apostles, by pouring fire out of our mouths in speaking truth to the world, leaving the outcome and our very protection to God.

At the 2017 Manning Centre Conference, controversial psychologist and author Jordan Peterson stated,

> Don't underestimate the power of truth. There is nothing more powerful. Now, in order to speak what you might regard as the truth, you have to let go of the outcome. You have to think, "All right I'm going to say what I think, stupid as I am, biased as I am, ignorant as I am. I'm going to state what I think, clearly as I can, and I'm going to live with the consequences, no matter what they are.
>
> …
>
> It's a price you want to pay if you're willing to believe that truth is the cornerstone of society, and in the most real sense. If you're willing to take that leap then tell the truth and see what happens. Nothing better could possibly happen to you. There'll be ups and downs, and there will be pushback, and it will be controversy—all of that. But it doesn't matter. The truth is what redeems the world from hell, and that's the truth.[16]

Jordan Peterson is not (yet) a Christian. However, his reading of Scripture and profound appreciation for the great authors and philosophers of the past has greatly impacted his thinking about truth, redemption, and our personal responsibilities in this world. As Peterson relates, it may not be safe or easy to speak the truth into a world of chaos. But it is precisely what we need to do, no matter the consequences.

War is bloody and brutal. I don't want to naïvely idealize it, but we simply cannot ignore the reality of the martial impetus in man. It is not only a component of our psyche, but a part of our obligation in a sin-stained world in which evil needs to be constantly pushed back lest Leviathans and Rahabs engulf the humble habitations of men like a great tidal wave. Today and increasingly in the days to come, we will

---

15   Or more accurately, the Spirit is sent by the Father through the Son.

16   Jordan P. Peterson, "2017/02/25: Postmodernism: Practice and Pathology," *YouTube*, https://www.youtube.com/watch?v=HzZ9h7bM6QE.

need a greater supply of warriors.

WHERE'S THE WARRIOR-CLASS?

I remember the first Final Fantasy video game that I played with my
friends on their Nintendo when it was released in the early '90s. Apparently the game was so named because it was intended to be Square's
last role-playing video game! In a happy irony, the series instead
went on to become one of the most successful videogame franchises
in history. For me, one of the most exciting aspects of role-playing
games is character selection and their subsequent development before
the game itself even starts. Sure, the story is good, and you want to
conquer the dragon, rescue the princess, or gain the treasure, whatever
the aim may be. But I have always most greatly enjoyed the process of
choosing what class of character I want to play, and then, depending
on the game, outfitting him with equipment, discovering his attributes,
or thinking through his skill-set—that is, to make him truly alive in
my mind. In the original Final Fantasy game, you could choose to be
one of six Light Warriors: a Fighter, Monk, Thief, White Mage, Black
Mage, or Red Mage. Leaving aside the question of how a black mage
can be a Light Warrior, or whether such a character is ethical for a
Christian to play, I was often drawn to the Fighter. If we were playing
with several friends, always boys, the Fighter never went unselected.

In real life too there is a class of fighters—men. Even in our
feminist-driven culture, it is hard to deny that men are built for battle.
Physically, men are faster, stronger, and more resilient. One highly
cited study found that men have 50% greater lower body strength and
66% greater upper body strength than women.[17] Male athletes are also
far less likely to be injured in competitive sports than their female
counterparts. Investigating a common athletic injury, one study stated that "the relative risk of concussion in collegiate female athletes
compared to male athletes has been reported to range from 53% higher
in basketball and 83% higher in soccer to 265% higher in baseball/

---

17   Ian Jannsen et al., "Skeletal Muscle Mass and Distribution in 468 Men and
Women Aged 18–88 Yr," *Journal of Applied Physiology* 89 (2000): 81–88.

softball."[18] A recent website advocating for the preservation of sex-seg-regated sports demonstrates the immense advantages that male athletes have over their female counterparts. It compares the athletes by sex and pretends to race together the 2016 finalists of track & field and swim-ming events. Unsurprisingly, the males dominate in these hypothetical races. In many cases almost *all* the women finish behind *all* the men. And if the sex differences were not clear enough, the comparison pre-sented is not between female and male Olympic finalists, but between female Olympic finalists and male *high-school* finalists.[19]

It is not merely physiology which separates the sexes and marks males as particularly suitable to be warriors. Men are far more willing to take risks, while women are more likely to be agreeable.[20] This general distinction emerges very early in life and is seen early in childhood play.[21] For instance, in responding to the wage-gap between men and women in society, Jordan Peterson has pointed out that among other awkward data that does not fit the liberal, feminist narrative, women are far less likely than men to ask or demand wage increases, an action that carries with it significant, if subtle ramifications.[22]

Even atheistic evolutionists will recognize the fittingness of many of these male-female asymmetries. Without significant con-straints on fertility, women are likely, on average, to spend many years with small children, and increasing numbers of them. The mother and her children are in a vulnerable state, and it makes sense that the father is able to protect and provide for them.[23] Feminists may decry

---

18   Cindy Lin, "Sex Differences in Common Sports Injuries," *Physical Medicine & Rehabilitation* 10, no. 10 (2018): 1073–82, https://doi.org/10.1016/j.pmrj.2018.03.008.

19   Jake Teater, "Boys vs Women," *BoysvsWomen*, 2020, https://boysvswomen.com/.

20   Joan Meyers-Levy and Barbara Loken, "Revisiting Gender Differences: What We Know and What Lies Ahead," *Journal of Consumer Psychology* 25, no. 1 (2014): 129–49.

21   Melissa Hines, Mihaela Constantinescu, and Debra Spencer, "Early Andro-gen Exposure and Human Gender Development," *Biology of Sex Differences* 6, no. 3 (2015): 1–10, https://doi.org/10.1186/s13293-015-0022-1.

22   Channel 4 News, "Jordan Peterson Debate on the Gender Pay Gap, Campus Protests and Postmodernism," *YouTube*, 2018, https://www.youtube.com/watch?v=aMcjxSThD54.

23   Rob Henderson, "When Men Behave Badly—A Review," *Quillette*, 2021, https://quillette.com/2021/04/30/when-men-behave-badly-a-review/.

these truths, but empirical studies reinforce these generalizations, and ironically demonstrate that women are most attracted to men who are stereotypically masculine.[24] Nature dies hard.

Men are designed to express more greatly the strength and initiative of God. Because of sin, this often goes bad. The victims of sexual crimes are usually women, and the perpetrators are almost always men.[25] The more violent or sexually perverse the crime, the more likely it is to be almost exclusively committed by men.[26] The solution to masculinity gone wrong, however, is not to give up on masculinity, let alone to give up on men. Society is in desperate need of men who will use their God-given strength to serve and sacrifice according to their specification. This truth is captured by the apostle Paul when he states, "Be watchful, stand firm in the faith, act like men, be strong" (1 Cor 16:13). Men ought to take risks, be the watchman for their families, discipline their little troops, and subdue the earth.

In contrast, it seems that women have been among those at the forefront of declaring truth in our culture. I am willing not only to link arms with these warrior-women, but to thank and praise them. Thinking about the sorts of battles in which I have been engaged, I am thankful for Elizabeth Johnstone, Kaeley-Triller Harms, Beth Steltzer, Emily Zinos, and Candace Owens in the United States. Here in Canada, I have been blessed to witness the strength and courage of women like Meghan Murphy, Amy Hamm, Barbara Kay, Linda Blade, Laura-Lynn Tyler Thompson, and Kari Simpson. Perhaps we are in a Deborah moment (Jdg 4:8–9) in Western society. If so, I bless God for these Deborahs! There is one thing, however, I cannot do, and that is to acquiesce that this state of affairs constitutes an ideal. It is rather, I am convinced, a travesty. It ought to predominantly be men commanding the troops and laying their lives on the line.

---

24   Martin J Tovée et al., "Characteristics of Male Attractiveness for Women," *The Lancet* 353, no. 9163 (1999): 1500.

25   "Women are rarely seen in clinical and forensic settings for concerns pertaining to their sexual interests or misbehaviors." Samantha J. Dawson, Brittany A. Bannerman, and Martin L. Lalumière, "Paraphilic Interests," *Sexual Abuse: A Journal of Research and Treatment* 28, no. 1 (2016): 20–45, https://doi.org/10.1177/1079063214525645.

26   Dawson, Bannerman, and Lalumière "Paraphilic Interests".

The world is in desperate need of men to reclaim their roles as warriors defending hearth and home, speaking with their enemies in the gate (Ps 127:5), and willing to lay down their lives for those weaker or more vulnerable than they. This is what strength does—it serves and sacrifices: "Husbands, love your wives, as Christ loved the church and gave himself up for her" (Eph 5:25). Instead, masculinity is generally demeaned in mainstream media as "toxic" while rarely are positive masculine traits or examples upheld. Is it any wonder that men are increasingly checking out on the mothers of their children and that boys increasingly lock themselves in their rooms where they can engage in war and sex without having to brave the bumps and bruises of reality?

Our churches need to be recruitment centers for a spiritual battle that very often spills out upon the earth. Our homes need to be training grounds so that our children know how to wear armour and use their sword. Our schools need to be arenas where a new generation of gladiators can spar with one another, grow their muscles, and feel some pains before they are thrust into open battle with the dragons and beasts of this world.[27] Women need much of this training too. But boys and men are in especial need of having a battle-scarred captain look into their eyes and say, "there is a great war that requires your blood. Let me put a sword in your hand."

REASONS FOR OPTIMISM

At all times there are battles to be fought, but hostilities are currently increasing in the world as dark powers are gaining ascendancy. As mentioned previously, the scriptures foretell that there will come a time in which these evil authorities are permitted by God to rule the world for a short while.

> [The beast] was allowed to make war on the saints and to conquer them. And authority was given it over every tribe and people and language and nation, and all who dwell on earth will worship it, everyone whose name has not been written before the foundation of

---

27   I will argue later in chapter three that for most families this will require homeschooling or Christian schooling.

the world in the book of life of the Lamb who was slain. If anyone has an ear, let him hear: If anyone is to be taken captive, to captivity he goes; if anyone is to be slain with the sword, with the sword must he be slain. Here is a call for the endurance and faith of the saints. (Rv 13:7–10)

How can the saint persevere without fear or anxiety in the midst of these sorts of trials, especially when he sees the immense size, power, or outright evil of our foes? How can he keep from succumbing to the lies which the Deceiver whispers to keep us from acquiring and using our spiritual weaponry: "the battle lies outside your purview," "the war is too costly," "no one else is fighting," "this is a battle you cannot win."

In J. R. R. Tolkien's *The Two Towers*, many of the original company who set out with Frodo to protect the ring of power find themselves alongside Théoden, King of Rohan, defending the stronghold of Helm's Deep from an enormous horde of orcs and evil men which outnumber them several times. In spite of feats of valour and prowess by Legolas, Gimli, and others, the defenders are forced back until they hold only the inner keep of the Hornburg. It is Aragorn who repeatedly keeps the men from despair, pointing to the hope that lies in the dawn of the new day.

King Théoden is not as hopeful of victory, but he is courageous, refusing to die in a defensive position. "'The end will not be long... But I will not end here, taken like an old badger in a trap. Snowmane and Hasufel and horses of my guard are in the inner court. When dawn comes, I will bid men sound Helm's horn, and I will ride forth. Will you ride with me then, son of Arathorn?'... 'I will ride with you,'" Aragorn returned.[28] So at dawn they rode out, and cut down swaths of the enemy in their mounted glory. It was only then that Gandalf the white wizard, a Christ figure in the book, arrived with another army, and the battle was won. Although help was already on the way, those inside the keep had to exit the stronghold and fight—it was then that victory came.

---

28   J.R.R. Tolkien, *The Two Towers* (London: HarperCollinsPublishers, 1999), 171.

Like those defenders looking down upon an innumerable foe or huddled together in the inner stronghold, there may be times we are similarly tempted to lose heart. Let me suggest several reasons to be courageous and take up our sword in hope of victory.

Firstly, we have certainty of the final outcome of the battle because Christ has already overcome death and the devil in His resurrection from the dead. Our captain states, "In the world you will have tribulation. But take heart, I have overcome the world" (Jn 16:33). Christ came to the earth to cast out the ruler of this world (Jn 12:31) and "to destroy the works of the devil" (1 Jn 3:8). In the book of Revelation it is no accident that the terrifying prophecies of the Dragon and beasts takes place only after the Lion of Judah has been given authority over all of history: "Weep no more; behold, the Lion of the tribe of Judah, the Root of David, has conquered, so that he can open the scroll and its seven seals" (Rv 5:5). Embattled saints, whether in the first or twenty-first century, are called to courage because we ultimately know who wins.

Secondly, we can take comfort in the sovereign control of God Almighty over all things, including over the Devil and his minions upon the earth. Even as nations and kings cast away the rule of God and reject the anointed Son, the one who sits in the heavens laughs at their pitiful plans because of His unassailable might and unstoppable purposes (Ps 2:4). There have been many upheavals in the past in which the nations have been shaken and great beastly powers have risen to test God's people. These events were all determined by the sovereign Lord who ordains all things. Even the mightiest historical empires—Babylon and Persia—were chosen by God and brought to ruin when His purposes for their empires were done. In a passage that forms part of the Old Testament basis of later prophecy in Revelation, Jeremiah foretells,

> Behold, like a lion coming up from the thicket of the Jordan against a perennial pasture, I will suddenly make them run away from her, and I will appoint over her whomever I choose. For who is like me? Who will summon me? What shepherd can stand before me? Therefore hear the plan that the LORD has made against Babylon, and the purposes that he has formed against the land of the Chaldeans:

Surely the little ones of their flock shall be dragged away; surely their fold shall be appalled at their fate. At the sound of the capture of Babylon the earth shall tremble, and her cry shall be heard among the nations. (Jer 50:44–46)

It is on account of the absolute power and control of God that we can be certain that victory will one day be ours as well.

This leads us, thirdly, to the crown that awaits those who conquer. We may not always win in the Senate or the law courts, but we are promised that not only will we preserve our lives by engaging in the battle, but that we will earn eternal glory from it as well. To the church of Smyrna who faced prison and tribulation, John not only wrote that "the one who conquers will not be hurt by the second death," but that if they were faithful unto death they would be given "the crown of life" (Rv 2:10–11). We ought to be motivated by the honour of our Lord and the glory we will share with Him forever. This eternal reward will make the sufferings of this present time incomparably small (Rom 8:18). In the words of King Théoden to Aragorn just prior to their final sortie at Helm's Deep, "Maybe we shall cleave a road, or make such an end as will be worth a song – if any be left to sing of us hereafter."[29]

VICTORY SONGS

Champions and victories call for song. The righteous ought to rejoice when evil is vanquished, Solomon states (Prv 11:10). When King David returned from hacking off Goliath's head, the women took out tambourines and sang in chorus together (1 Sam 18:7). When God brought the Red Sea back upon the tyrannous Egyptians, Israel praised the Lord for being a "man of war" (Ex 15:1–3). And in Revelation, at the destruction of debauched Babylon, a great multitude shouts "Hallelujah" as they are avenged (Rv 19:1–3). These songs serve not only as joyous remembrances of faith-filled heroes and the help of God, but function to instill courage for the battles which remain.

---

29   Tolkien, *The Two Towers*, 171.

Early on in my ministry as a lead pastor, a mature believer suggested that as Pastor I ought to open our services with an invocation from God's Word. To my shame we were not doing this at the time, as it was not part of our denominational tradition. Since then, we have begun every meeting with an invocation from Scripture, usually from the Psalms. Among the benefits of regular congregational reading of the Psalms is that you cannot fail to miss the struggle and the warfare in its verses. Sometimes I internally wince as I read the invocation as I wonder how some visitor will interpret those martial phrasings in the Psalms which appear alongside their words of comfort and encouragement. Nevertheless, the practice of reading them publicly has reenforced for me, and I trust for our church, the reality of the battle, the need to engage in it, and what our response ought to be.

These were songs to be sung; they were also prayers to be prayed. I suspect we only have the slightest inkling of the degree to which our prayers may be weapons against the enemy. The account of Rees Howells and his band of intercessors is one tantalizing example. If the title of "prayer-warrior" applies to anyone in history, it applies to Howells. Born in 1879 in Wales,[30] he experienced the remarkable revival there in 1904,[31] but he also saw the devastation of two World Wars. Throughout his life, the Lord developed him into a radical, faith-filled person of prayer and he witnessed many miracles as a result. Chief among them may have been the outcome of his intercession for the Allies in World War II. Howells had come to believe already by March 1936 that Hitler was an agent of Satan.[32] In his biography of the intercessor, Norman Grubb relates how he and his band of intercessors prayed day by day for military theatres and operations like Dunkirk, Alexandria, Salerno, and D-Day.[33] Although issue could be taken with Howell's propensity to predict outcomes (and sometimes get them wrong), it is hard to escape the conclusion that this group of

---

30   Norman Grubb, *Rees Howells, Intercessor* (Fort Washington, PA: CLC Publications, 2016), 13.

31   Grubb, *Rees Howells,* 34.

32   Grubb, *Rees Howells,* 291.

33   Grubb, *Rees Howells,* 291–322.

prayer-warriors may have been responsible for the overthrow of Hitler and the Beast-like Third Reich.

In light of Christ's command to love our enemies, some may ask whether it is permissible to pray curses upon unrepentantly evil rulers. The answer from the Psalms is that we *must* pray curses on these anti-Christ figures. We must first pray for their blessing and salvation. But if they refuse to bow the knee to the Lord, the church is to join together and ask for heaven to deal its avenging blows upon those who stand opposed to Christ's dominion. We must read, sing, and pray the "War Psalms of the Prince of Peace," to borrow the title of James Adams' helpful book on the imprecatory Psalms. In his conclusion, he cites Cornelius Van Til, "It is at all times a part of the task of the people of God to destroy evil. Once we see this we do not, for instance, meanly apologize for the imprecatory psalms, but glory in them."[34] We need to stop apologizing for the good and the true.

Do Not Apologize for Truth

I remember the call from the local TV news station. I was out enjoying my day off with my family, meandering in the city as we looked for a piece of furniture for the house. Would I be willing to be interviewed about my anti-Bill C-16 posters that afternoon? I suspected my views would be misinterpreted and my interview carefully edited according to the prevailing liberal bias of the day. I could have said "no." It was my day off, after all. And I was not sure I was ready for an escalation in the war. But I had started something, and could I really back out now? I made a choice that day—I would always be willing to speak to the media. There have been times I have faltered, not speaking as precisely as I would have wanted. But I have learned. And not only to speak—to use the sword of truth—but I have also learned something of the nature of these little skirmishes. They are tests.

One of the most effective tactics evil powers use in our world, and I see this particularly in Canada, is to advance until those on the

---

34   James E. Adams, *War Psalms of the Prince of Peace*, Second (Phillipsburg, NJ: P & R Pub., 2016), 101.

side of good plant their flag in the ground and say, "no further—this is my hill and I will die upon it rather than give another inch." It is astonishing how often victories are won merely by refusing to back down. If you speak truth, do not apologize; double down. Learn to speak winsomely, graciously, and calmly, but do not leave your "sword" in its sheath. It is not merely murderers, sorcerers, and the sexually immoral who will be refused entrance to the glory of the King and His eternal city, but also the cowardly: "But as for the cowardly, the faithless, the detestable, as for murderers, the sexually immoral, sorcerers, idolaters, and all liars, their portion will be in the lake that burns with fire and sulfur, which is the second death" (Rv 21:8).

The book of Revelation begins with seven calls to "conquer." Only with a mind and heart set upon the martial nature of life is one ready to deal with the tribulations of this life. Similarly, the exhortation of this first chapter to take up arms in the struggle against chaos and evil is foundational to everything else we will consider. The other principles will not work if we are weak-willed, shirk our responsibilities, or are unwilling to engage in battle. We must declare the message of God fully—not only His love for the world, but His judgment against the sins of our world and culture. We must uphold and apply Christ's standard of justice in the marketplaces and institutions of our world as a prophetic people. The call is issued by our captain: warriors wanted. The struggle starts with buying a "sword".

Apocalypse-Preparation List

- Embrace adventure and struggle in your life. Be willing to sustain some wounds for what is most important.
- Do not be silent at work, in the marketplace, or online. Your words are your "sword."
- Men—embrace your special role as warriors in protecting your family and neighbours from evil. Boys—learn to speak, have courage, and follow Dad into battle.
- Recognize the war is already won by Christ and that God is in control. Do not be fearful or anxious. You will win if you are on the side of the triumphant Lamb.
- Learn to pray the imprecations of Scripture against God's enemies, even as you continue to pray for their salvation.
- When you do not "win" right away, do not back down. And if you have done nothing wrong, do not be cowed into apologizing for the truth.
- Memorize Psalm 18:29–34. "For by you I can run against a troop, and by my God I can leap over a wall. This God—his way is perfect; the word of the LORD proves true; he is a shield for all those who take refuge in him. For who is God, but the LORD? And who is a rock, except our God?— the God who equipped me with strength and made my way blameless. He made my feet like the feet of a deer and set me secure on the heights. He trains my hands for war, so that my arms can bend a bow of bronze."

CHAPTER 2

Flee the Carnival

LIVING IN THE AMUSEMENT PARK

In Carlo Collodi's famous *Adventures of Pinocchio*, the puppet is just a day away from the fulfillment of his wish to become a real boy when he is lured and enticed by his friend Candlewick. Candlewick revels as he describes to Pinocchio a fantasy island in which there are no schools, no masters, and no studies. The days "are spent in play and amusement from morning till night. When night comes you go to bed, and recommence the same life in the morning."[1] Pinocchio, who had promised to be good, tries to withstand the pressure, but when the carriage comes to take the boys away to this magical place, he succumbs. There is no more room in the carriage itself and so he mounts a donkey and immediately hears a voice cry out,

> Bear it in mind, simpleton! Boys who refuse to study and turn their backs upon books, schools and masters, to pass their time in play and amusement, sooner or later come to a bad end. I know it by experience, and I can tell you. A day will come when you will weep as I am weeping now, but then it will be too late![2]

Pinocchio fails to heed the warning from the poor beast of burden and in the end is transformed into a donkey himself. Although he suffers much, he is eventually delivered by his personal saviour, a very gracious fairy. The story is instructive and perhaps never more so than

---

1   Carlo Collodi, *Pinocchio: The Tale of a Puppet* (Racine, WI: Whitman, 1916), chap. 30, https://www.gutenberg.org/files/16865/16865-h/16865-h.htm.

2   Collodi, *Pinocchio,* chap. 30.

now. A life spent seeking diversion will result in much suffering, and for many people in our world the results will be far worse than they were for Collodi's little puppet.

Jesus responds in Luke 17:20–37 to the question of when the kingdom of God would come. In a passage that contains considerable warnings of not only a spiritual but also a practical nature, He gives the examples of judgment in the days of both Noah and Lot. In both cases, He observes that people were carrying on their lives as if it were any other day—eating and drinking and carrying on social life and commerce (v27–28). Beyond the element of surprise, however, there is another aspect to Christ's warning—they are told to flee without regard to the luxuries and comforts they have accumulated in this life: "On that day, let the one who is on the housetop, with his goods in the house, not come down to take them away, and likewise let the one who is in the field not turn back. Remember Lot's wife. Whoever seeks to preserve his life will lose it, but whoever loses his life will keep it" (v31–33).

The example of Sodom and Gomorrah is fit for Jesus' purposes here not only because the city was wicked and fell suddenly under God's judgment, but also because they were wealthy and licentious. The wealth of the valley region was the reason Lot chose to dwell there in the first place (Gn 13:10), and Christ implies that Sodom's life of luxury and ease was partly why Lot's wife looked back longingly at the city—and was instantly turned into a pillar of salt (Gn 19:26).

Recent revisionists, hoping to rid the Bible of its clear condemnations of homosexual practice, have argued that the sin for which Sodom and Gomorrah were judged was not homosexuality but inhospitality and excess.[3] Although this revisionism simply does not stand up to the scrutiny of Scripture,[4] there is nevertheless an important sense in which Sodom's wealth and luxurious living created a feeding

---

3   Matthew Vines, *God and the Gay Christian* (Convergent Books, 2014), 59–76.

4   James Hamilton, "How to Condone What the Bible Condemns: Matthew Vines Takes on the Old Testament," *For His Renown*, 2014, https://jimhamilton. info/2014/04/25/how-to-condone-what-the-bible-condemns-matthew-vines-takes-on-the-old-testament/.

frenzy for their flesh in multiple ways—sexual and physical: "Behold, this was the guilt of your sister Sodom: she and her daughters had pride, excess of food, and prosperous ease, but did not aid the poor and needy. They were haughty and did an abomination before me. So I removed them, when I saw it" (Ez 16:49–50). Sodom was judged for sexual immorality; they were also judged for excess of food.

THEIR GOD IS THEIR BELLY

We live in a prosperous age. To the average person in twenty-first century North America or Europe, it is difficult to comprehend the incredible changes to our food supply which have taken place in recent history, both in terms of abundance and diversity. In *Blood, Iron and Gold*, Christian Wolmar details how railway expansion in the 1800s completely revolutionized food supply: "Almost overnight, with the opening of a line, fresh food became available from the countryside."[5] Until then, there had been no reliable way to get fresh produce from the outlying farmlands into the cities. Within the space of a couple decades, all of that changed. For most of history, man has been dependent on the seasons as the determinative factor for what they could eat and when. The miracles of industrialization and international shipping allow us to now access the foods we enjoy almost all year long. Feasts used to be annual or bi-annual community events associated with harvest-time in which God or gods were praised and thanked. Now, we feast almost every night, on almost anything we want, often all alone, and without a hint of true thankfulness.

In Euripides' *The Cyclops*, the great one-eyed monster and antagonist boasts about his sensuality to the hero Odysseus, stating, "The earth perforce, whether she like it or not, produces grass and fattens my flocks, which I sacrifice to no one save myself and this belly, the greatest of deities."[6] Over four hundred years later, the apostle Paul

5   Christine Wolmar, *Blood, Iron, and Gold* (New York: PublicAffairs, 2009), 225.

6   Euripides, *The Cyclops*, trans. E. P. Coleridge, http://classics.mit.edu/Euripides/cyclops.html.

wrote, "Their end is destruction, their god is their belly, and they glory in their shame, with minds set on earthly things" (Phil 3:19). This idea may seem like nothing more than hyperbole—a shocking statement meant only for the most gluttonous among us. The reality is much more sobering.

Consider the ending of the gospel of John which appears in many respects as an epilogue. There seems to be a fitting ending to the book already in the last few verses of chapter 20 in which doubting Thomas finally sees and believes in the risen Christ who states, "Bless-ed are those who have not seen and yet have believed." Immediately following, there is a closing purpose statement for the book in John 20:30–31. It seems like the perfect place to end a glorious account of Christ's life. Clearly, however, John thought otherwise.[7]

The account that follows is of a breakfast on the shores of Galilee. Peter and six other disciples are out fishing and, in an echo of a previous event (Lk 5:1–11), they catch nothing until a stranger on the shore shouts to them to throw their net on the other side of the boat. Their obedience yields an enormous haul of fish. They recognize the stranger on the shore as Christ, and Peter, with characteristic zeal, jumps in and wades to shore, reaching the Lord first. Jesus is already preparing a breakfast of fish and bread for them at a charcoal fire, pro-viding the same two elements as in the feeding of the five thousand (Jn 6:1–15). This echo is very deliberate, as we shall see.

When they finish breakfast, Jesus asks Peter, who had denied Him three times in the courtyard of the high priest prior to His cruci-fixion, "Simon, son of John, do you love me more than these?" There is significance in the fact that Jesus asks virtually the same question—"do you love me"—three times, to which Peter responds three times in the affirmative. These three affirmations undo the three denials, and publicly reinstate this fallen leader.

The initial framing of the question as a comparison, however, has puzzled commentators, and resulted in several interpretations. The

---

7   John may have several good reasons for the final chapter of his gospel account. Writing much later than the other gospels, he also wants to clear up miscon-ceptions about his own life and likely even his relationship with Peter, who figures so prominently in the epilogue.

first is that "these" refers to the other disciples—does Peter love Jesus more than he loves his fishing buddies? Relatively few scholars take this view. The second, and most widely held interpretation, is that the comparison is between Peter's love for Jesus and the other disciples' love for Jesus. Although possible, it seems an unfitting comparison on the lips of our Lord, especially in light of the disciples' prior jealousies (Mt 20:20–28, Lk 9:46–48) and this very public reinstatement.[8] The last option, which may seem unlikely at first glance, is that Jesus is asking whether Peter loves Him more than he loves the fish.[9] I understand those who scoff at this interpretation as a legitimate option. Rationally, who would possibly love food more than He who is God Himself—the good and gracious—the self-giving one? The answer is deeply troubling.

After the earlier feeding of the five thousand in John 5, the people following Jesus were flabbergasted. Here was a man who could solve the poverty of the nation. Perhaps of the entire world! They wanted to see more and eat more, and so when Jesus miraculously stole over the water at night they got in their boats and followed Him to the other side of the Sea of Galilee. When they caught up to the miracle-worker, Jesus confronted them and their bellies. In the teaching that follows, He compares Himself to the manna with which God fed them in the wilderness, saying that He is the Bread of Life. Pointing symbolically to how faith must appropriate its object—to ingest it, as it were—Jesus tells them that "unless you eat the flesh of the Son of Man and drink his blood, you have no life in you" (Jn 6:53). Whether it was the bizarre language or merely the challenge to true faith which was the precipitating event, the crowds and even many of Jesus' followers turned back at that point (Jn 6:66). They preferred fish and

---

8   Jesus would be asking Peter if he loved Him more than the other disciples loved Him in front of the other disciples.

9   See Craig S. Keener, *The Gospel According to John, Vol. 2* (Peabody, MA: Hendrickson, 2003), 1236. One of the supports for this interpretation from the immediate context is the sheer frequency of the word "fish" in verses one to fourteen. Stephen J. Smith argues that this and other phonetically-related repetitions would have been far more obvious to native Greek speakers hearing the passage read aloud. Stephen J Smith, "Phonology, Fish, and the Form ToytΩn : A New Aproach to an Old Crux in John 21," *JETS* 62, no. 4 (2019): 739–48.

bread to eternal life in Christ! But the story does not end there. Jesus then turned to the Twelve and asked them if they too wanted to leave. Peter, bold as always, stated that in spite of Christ's challenging words, he would not leave Jesus like these others had. As we know, however, he eventually did. And he did so as he stood warming his hands at a charcoal fire.[10]

And so now in John's epilogue, around a charcoal fire on a beach of the Sea of Galilee, Jesus is once more saying to Peter, by comparing Himself to the fish, "follow me and leave the world and the desires of the flesh." It may seem logically unbelievable that anyone would choose fish or food over the eternal Bread of Heaven, but the whole history of man and his sins demonstrates this terrible truth. Adam and Eve traded the eternal blessedness of God to partake of the fruit of the one tree they were forbidden (Gn 3:6). Esau sold his inheritance from God to his brother Jacob for only a lentil stew (Gn 25:34). And then you have the "disciples" of John 6 who fell away instead of embracing the larger realities to which the food pointed.

Easy Does It (In)

Food is just one example of how creature comforts tempt us to build our homes here in this world, rather than with Christ in the next. Comfort, ease, and entertainment form the context in which we live. More problematically yet, they form pursuits, even for many so-called Christians. This reality makes us extremely vulnerable to the siren-song of the perpetual carnival which leads to destruction. In *Pinocchio,* the puppet is on the verge of becoming truly human when he succumbs to Candlewick's temptation of a life of amusement and instead of becoming a boy, he is transformed into a donkey. Diversion and dissipation have a dehumanizing effect on the life of man. The pursuit of entertainment drains our lives of that which makes us truly human.

We were created to be little gods, tasked with the glorious duty of fashioning this world to reflect our Creator. Instead, many spend

---

10   These are the only two times this Greek word translated "charcoal fire" is used in the New Testament.

their days, or at least their non-working hours, consuming endless drivel in artificial and purposeless pursuits. In his modern classic, *Amusing Ourselves to Death*, Neil Postman chronicles how the rise of television utterly transformed the way people think and interact with the world. He argues that the problem is not that we sought mindlessness through this new visual medium, but that through television, mindlessness entered into *every* sphere. As Polish philosophy professor Ryszard Legutko observes,

> In today's world entertainment is not just a pastime or a style, but a substance that permeates everything: schools and universities, upbringing of children, intellectual life, art, morality, and religion. It has become dear to the hearts of student, professors, entrepreneurs, journalists, engineers, scientists, writers, even priests. Entertainment imposes itself psychologically, intellectually, socially, and also, strange as it may sound, spiritually. A failure to provide human endeavours—even the most noble ones—with an entertaining wrapping is today unthinkable and borders on sin.[11]

This everything-as-entertainment culture has a dehumanizing effect on man. We become donkeys, feeding on fodder, jumping through predetermined hoops, and incapable of mature living. Many are content to consume rather than build, to view rather than think, to play rather than work. Responsibilities are traded for handouts and purpose is traded for passing pleasure. According to Pew Research, US teens spend roughly an hour a day on homework, but more than three hours per day on leisure screen-time.[12] American adults' daily average time spent reading books (11 min) is dwarfed by the hours spent watching television (3 hr 30 min) or engaging with digital social media (1 hr 10 min).[13] Apologist Andy Steiger reflects on the role technology

11   Ryszard Legutko, *The Demon in Democracy* (New York: Encounter Books, 2018), 36.

12   Gretchen Livingston, "The Way U.S. Teens Spend Their Time Is Changing, but Differences Between Boys and Girls Persist," *Pew Resarch Center*, 2019, https://www.pewresearch.org/fact-tank/2019/02/20/the-way-u-s-teens-spend-their-time-is-changing-but-differences-between-boys-and-girls-persist/.

13   Audrey Schomer, "US Adults Will Consume Almost As Much Media in 2021, but TV Viewing Will Backslide," *Insider Intelligence*, 2021, https://www.insiderintelligence.com/content/us-adults-will-consume-almost-much-media-2021-tv-viewing-will-backslide.

plays in what he calls the "outsourcing" of our humanity.[14]

> We attempt to fulfill those human longings while keeping our focus on ourselves, and technology makes that possible. Don't want the hassle of dating, the challenges of marriage, or the career-killer of children? Technology promises to solve all of our relational needs quickly, conveniently, and hassle free. Need a friend? There's social media and chatbots for that? Need intimacy? There's pornography and robot sex for that. Want a child? There's a video game for that, even an app to see what they would look like and virtual goggles to interact with them. Is it working? Is this leading to greater human flourishing? Is our technology making us more human or less?[15]

Is it any wonder that there is an epidemic of anxiety in the Western world?[16] We long for meaning, but stuck in a cocoon of self-selected entertainment and assuaged by increasingly lowered standards for what defines a successful life, many people have never built resiliency or discovered a purpose which can only be attained through the struggles of real life. This dehumanization is lamentable in all people, although it is more understandable among those who do not know Christ and the eternal purposes found in Him. How much more serious is this state when it is found among those who have been saved from an empty way of life handed down to us by our fathers in the flesh (1 Pt 1:18).

ENTERTAINMENT ENSLAVEMENT

In an entertainment-pursuit culture, dehumanization is followed by enslavement. This is illustrated in the story of Pinocchio who is sold, ironically, to a circus, where his stable is a prison and he is made to do tricks by the force of the whip.

In his disturbing dystopian novel, *Brave New World*, Aldous

---

14   Andy Steiger, *Reclaimed* (Grand Rapids, MI: Zondervan Reflective, 2020), 101.

15   Steiger, *Reclaimed*, 94. We will return to this question in the next chapter as we consider the rehabilitation and centrality of the renewed mind in human agency.

16   James Innes-Smith, "The Truth About the Anxiety Epidemic," *The Spectator*, March 23, 2022, https://www.spectator.co.uk/article/the-truth-about-the-anxiety-epidemic/.

Huxley tells of a world dominated by consumerism and ease, with just enough work to keep society functioning. Near the end of the book, the director, one of few people with power in the society, has just finished reading a scholarly essay that is a bit too true to be published. The director, reflecting, concludes,

> It was a masterly piece of work. But once you began admitting explanations in terms of purpose—well, you didn't know what the result might be. It was the sort of idea that might easily recondition the more unsettled minds among the higher castes—make them lose their faith in happiness as the Sovereign Good and take to believing, instead, that the goal was somewhere beyond, somewhere outside the human sphere; that the purpose of life was not the maintenance of well-being, but some intensification and refining of consciousness, some enlargement of knowledge.[17]

Unlike the top-down totalitarianism in George Orwell's *1984*, Huxley's *Brave New World* keeps civilization enslaved not by coercion, but by pleasure-seeking. Writing twenty years after its first release, he stated,

> A really efficient totalitarian state would be one in which the all-powerful executive of political bosses and their army of managers control a population of slaves who do not have to be coerced, because they love their servitude. To make them love it is the task assigned, in present-day totalitarian states, to ministers of propaganda, newspaper editors and school-teachers.[18]

In our day this very thing is taking place subtly through technological platforms and applications. Just a few months prior to writing this book I had a conversation with a good friend who agreed that there are totalitarian trajectories in our culture for which we need to prepare. I told him that one small part of diagnosing my life's dependency on the world is to move away from services associated with Google and its platforms, including Gmail, their ubiquitous and free email service. He looked at me and said, "I don't know how I would even begin to do that!"

---

17   Aldous Huxley, *Brave New World* (Toronto: Vintage Canada, 2007), 154.

18   Huxley, *Brave New World,* xxiii.

Companies are not in the business of giving things away for free. They exist to make money. I have no intrinsic problem with this motivation. I continue to believe in free market principles, its warts and weaknesses notwithstanding. With the proliferation of internet-connected devices and the applications which run on them, however, new ground is constantly being broken in the technological sphere—along with centuries-old societal contracts. It has often been stated that if a service or platform offers you something for free, that "you are the product." In *The Age of Surveillance Capitalism*, however, Shoshana Zuboff explains that this idiom is insufficient to describe contemporary techno-capitalism and that the modern reality is far, far worse.

> Surveillance capitalism's products and services are not the objects of a value exchange. They do not establish constructive producer-consumer reciprocities. Instead, they are the "hooks" that lure users into their extractive operations in which our personal experiences are scraped and packaged as the means to others' ends. We are not surveillance capitalism's "customers." Although the saying tells us "If it's free, then you are the product," that is also incorrect. We are the sources of surveillance capitalism's crucial surplus: the objects of a technologically advanced and increasingly inescapable raw-material-extraction operation.[19]

These "hooks" are extensive and they make extricating oneself from surveillance capitalism's almost universal dominion very painful. We will return to the idea of surveillance itself later, as the idea of a universal, AI-driven "Big Other" having access to widespread and intimate personal knowledge about us has serious implications worth further reflection. For now, we want to merely consider the fact of this pervasive enslavement.

Reflect for a second upon what it would cost you to give up using Apple or Google services. If it were proven that a given technological giant was not only subtly immoral, but flagrantly so, and boldly anti-Christ, could you leave its grip? Could you stop using Gmail, Google Docs, Google Maps, Google Translate? Could you give up Facebook

---

19   Zuboff, *The Age of Surveillance Capitalism*, 10.

with its digital network of friendship and its stable of applications like Instagram and WhatsApp? Could you live without a cellphone? Or at the very least, are you ready to pay four times the price for one that is not ethically compromised?[20] These are the decisions that in all likelihood we will be forced to make in the very near future.

For many people, the proverbial frog-in-the-pot will continue to slowly boil. From mainstream media sources there will be no notice of lines being crossed, of inherent dangers in continual use, or of gross ethical concerns about these tech platforms. It will be business as normal while we feed our own enslavement. The apostle Paul puts down as a principle that we must not be dominated by anything (1 Cor 6:12). Peter likewise states that "whatever overcomes a person, to that he is enslaved (2 Pt 2:19). These principles are more than mere wisdom for living, although they are not less than that. They are fundamental axioms of the Christian life. It is for freedom that Christ has set us free, and so any master that is not God is to be rejected and thrown off (Gal 5:1). If there is *anything* which controls you—you need to give it up. If Google or Apple have mastery over your life—you need to leave that tyrant. If you could not do without your cellphone—it is time to put it away until you can. If it is food or coffee or the television, whatsoever it may be, you *must* learn to be able to live without it. The evil powers of the world are betting that you will not be able to.

WHO IS MARKING YOU?

We briefly considered the mark of the Beast in the first chapter, and I want to return to it now to consider its practical warning. Echoing some of the language of the prophet Daniel, Revelation 13 tells of a first beast who is given authority by God for a specific amount of time during which he blasphemes God and makes war, quite successfully, against the saints (v7). His dominion will be universal and all the peoples of the earth, with a crucial exception, will worship the Beast. A second beast, also called the False Prophet, rises from the earth,

---

20   We will examine ethical concerns further in chapter six.

does great signs, deceives the nations, and "causes all, both small and great, both rich and poor, both free and slave, to be marked on the right hand or the forehead, so that no one can buy or sell unless he has the mark, that is, the name of the beast or the number of its name" (Rv 13:16–17).

The ominous nature of the prophecy notwithstanding, there is important context to this mark earlier in Revelation. In chapter seven, 144,000 from twelve tribes of Israel, a highly symbolic number applied to a highly symbolic tribal list,[21] are "sealed on their foreheads," in a very clear parallel to the later Mark of the Beast. This righteous seal is mentioned later in Revelation 9:4, 14:1, and 22:4, and is a well-developed theme throughout the book.[22] The idea of a notable, publicly visible marking is not unique to Revelation, either. It has its roots firmly in the first story of redemption in Exodus 13:9: "And it shall be to you as a sign on your hand and as a memorial between your eyes, that the law of the LORD may be in your mouth. For with a strong hand the LORD has brought you out of Egypt" (Ex 13:9). Ezekiel 9 also serves as an important parallel to this marking of the righteous.

> And the LORD said to him, "Pass through the city, through Jerusalem, and put a mark on the foreheads of the men who sigh and groan over all the abominations that are committed in it." And to the others he said in my hearing, "Pass through the city after him, and strike. Your eye shall not spare, and you shall show no pity. Kill old men outright, young men and maidens, little children and women, but touch no one on whom is the mark. (Ez 9:4–6)

This background is crucial for understanding the mark of the Beast in Revelation. There are many Christians who are anxious or fearful about this mark. Their alertness is helpful, but in many cases their interest or caution is directed too specifically. Just as the seal upon the righteous is symbolic of true, living faith, so too the Beast's mark is

---

21   The very unusual list argues strongly against the interpretation that this group is ethnic Israel. Dennis Johnson, *Triumph of the Lamb* (Phillipsburg, NJ: P & R Pub., 2001), 130–33.

22   This last reference is helpful because it communicates, if it were not already clear, that the "sealed" are not a select group, like the martyrs, but represent all God's people: "the throne of God and of the Lamb will be in it [New Jerusalem], and his servants will worship him."

symbolic of an embrace of the world-system, and its inherent hostility to the dominion of Christ. This mark has been manifested in many ways throughout the centuries, including the burning of incense to Caesar in the early church and the oath of allegiance to Hitler in Nazi Germany.

This is not to say that there will not be a very physical "mark" in the future. In fact, I will note in the last chapter the likelihood of a future global, biometric digital identification, and how some very powerful companies and organizations would like to see this ID manifested as an implant. This may or may not come to pass in the near future. The traps, however, are being laid now through society's wholehearted, unthinking, and naïve acceptance of comfort, entertainment, and ease-granting technological platforms.

Like Pinocchio, our world is increasingly being dehumanized as we eschew mature, God-glorifying responsibility, and is being enslaved by the circus in which we desire to live. Sadly, unlike in Collodi's parable, many people are completely content with their imprisonment in this brave new world.

FIGHTING THE FLESH

The scriptures, however, give us practical strategies to keep us from the tempting lure of the circus. In the Sermon on the Mount, Christ's kingdom-manifesto, He mentions several disciplines that were well recognized, but wrongly employed in His culture. In Matthew 6:1–4, Jesus speaks about financial giving that is done not to look good in other's eyes, but for God. Greed is a powerful desire that strengthens the hold this world and its pleasures have upon us. The apostle John warns,

> Do not love the world or the things in the world. If anyone loves the world, the love of the Father is not in him. For all that is in the world—the desires of the flesh and the desires of the eyes and pride of life—is not from the Father but is from the world. And the world is passing away along with its desires, but whoever does the will of God abides forever. (1 Jn 2:15–17)

Sacrificial charitable giving, the kind that C.S. Lewis suggests hurts at least a bit, is a powerful antidote to the temptations of our circus-world.[23] It is not difficult to flee the fire falling on Sodom or the destruction of Jerusalem (Mt 24:16) when one does not have much to leave behind! As Proverbs 13:8 states, "a poor man hears no threat."

It is standard Christian practice to give a tenth of all that we earn to God. I believe, however, that this is really just the beginning of Christian giving. Randy Alcorn, author of *Money, Possessions and Eternity*, calls tithing the "training wheels" of Christian giving,[24] and the examples which God holds out for our emulation in the New Testament often go much further than a tithe. The Macedonian churches, for instance, were commended for joyful generosity in "extreme poverty" (2 Cor 8:1–2).

There is a place for pleasure in this world—God gives us many good things to enjoy here (Eccl 5:18, 1 Tm 6:17). Furthermore, we ought to put our money to work in providing for our families (Prv 31, 1 Tm 5:8). But what I see increasingly in these prosperous days are Christians whose faith only barely creeps into their financial affairs and pocketbooks. Generous giving is not only a God-ordained means of supporting Christian work and missions, it is a powerful practice for keeping oneself free of the world's chains.

In the Sermon on the Mount, Jesus also mentions fasting. Once again, it was to be done in a certain manner and with the right motivation, not for show before men, but before the audience of heaven and He who sees and rewards. The disciples were not known for fasting while Christ was with them, but Jesus prophesied that the days were coming in which they would fast (Lk 5:35).

The practice of fasting has not only spiritual, but practical benefits as well. Of all the vivid pictures presented in Revelation, few

---

23   "I do not believe one can settle how much we ought to give. I am afraid the only safe rule is to give more than we can spare. In other words, if our expenditure on comforts, luxuries, amusements, etc, is up to the standard common among those with the same income as our own, we are probably giving away too little. If our charities do not at all pinch or hamper us, I should say they are too small." C.S. Lewis, *Mere Christianity* (New York: MacMillan Pub. Co., 1952), 81–82.

24   Randy Alcorn, *Money, Possessions, and Eternity* (Carol Strem, IL: Tyndale House Publishers, 2003), chap. 12. Alcorn's shorter book on the same subject, *The Treasure Principle*, is better known and also excellent.

are more notable than that of the Four Horsemen of the Apocalypse in chapter 6. Hidden within this section, however, is a curious verse describing an undesirable future in which a quart of wheat and three quarts of barley will each cost a denarius, but the oil and wine will be unharmed (Rv 6:6). It seems likely, given that the entire section describes the beginning of God's wrath, and that no other part of it describes anything positive, that even the protection of the oil and wine is, in some way, negative.

William Newell, writing in 1935, observed, "that the oil and wine are to be spared indicates, it seems, that the rich have their luxuries despite the terrible scarcity among the poor" and noted that even in his time "the whole movement of 'government' is to appropriate private property. See Russia, Italy, Germany, and the 'New Deal' in America. But the very rich are seen here as still having their luxuries, under this third seal, and the great mass ground to poverty."[25] I think Newell is right and that an incredible disparity between rich elites and poor plebeians will increase at the time of the end. Given that the Christian will not at that time be able to "buy or sell" without being marked as belonging to the Beast's system, we may need to pray more than ever, "give us today our daily bread" (Mt 6:11). Training our bodies by fasting will help us adapt to these realities both spiritually and physically.

A third spiritual practice underlying Christ's commands in Matthew 6 is contentment. Although not explicitly named, contentment would seem to be the positive corollary of prayer for our needs (Mt 6:11), seeking our reward in heaven rather than on earth (Mt 6:19–24), and not being anxious about food or clothing (Mt 6:25–34). I am thankful that I was raised by godly parents to be grateful for the food on our plates, to not waste, and to work if we expected to eat. Although we were not rich, and I sometimes fell into childhood covetousness of my friends' belongings, I am quite sure I never missed a meal, which is more than can be said for most people throughout history and many people today.

We are told in Scripture, "For we brought nothing into the

---

25   William R. Newell, *The Book of Revelation* (Chicago: Moody Press, 1935), 104.

world, and we cannot take anything out of the world. But if we have food and clothing, with these we will be content" (1 Tm 6:7–8). Do Christians really believe this? It seems to me that many in the church do not evidence this contentment with little and instead invest heavily in the world and their own kingdoms. But as they do so, many are building not only businesses, reputations, and homes here, but an apparatus of slavery—an unseen cage from which it will be increasingly difficult to escape. "Keep your life free from love of money," the writer of Hebrews exhorts, "and be content with what you have, for he has said, 'I will never leave you nor forsake you.' So we can confidently say, 'The Lord is my helper; I will not fear; what can man do to me?'" (Heb 13:5–6). It may be that in the days to come we will need to claim these promises like we never have before.

THE END OF THE CIRCUS

One of the more popular visions of an apocalyptic future in recent years is the young-adult book series, and its movie derivation, *The Hunger Games*. In it, twelve districts of common and poor citizenry are kept in check through a variety of means, including the eponymous games, in which all but one set of "players" die in a televised, gladiatorial spectacle. These districts, by their labour, supply a lavish lifestyle to the citizens of the central city, called Panem. The name Panem is from the Latin phrase "Panem et circenses"— "bread and circuses". The phrase is used to describe the means by which Roman rule used entertainment to keep the common people from more central concerns and rebellion. In his short tract, *The Politics of Obedience*, Etienne de la Boetie writes,

> Plays, farces, spectacles, gladiators, strange beasts, medals, pictures, and other such opiates, these were for ancient peoples the bait toward slavery, the price of their liberty, the instruments of tyranny. By these practices and enticements the ancient dictators so successfully lulled their subjects under the yoke, that the stupefied peoples, fascinated by the pastimes and vain pleasures flashed before their eyes, learned subservience as naively, but not so creditably, as

little children learn to read by looking at bright picture books.[26]

One day, however, the circus will come to an end and God will punish those who have made the carnival their life. The coming apocalypse will not be kind to those who have never matured, but like little children, have given themselves to easy pleasures, preferring food and games to Christ and the spiritual rewards of the kingdom of heaven. Revelation 18 contains the cries of the rich and luxury-laden upon seeing the destruction of their beloved Babylon, pictured as a bloodstained harlot.

> And the merchants of the earth weep and mourn for her, since no one buys their cargo anymore, cargo of gold, silver, jewels, pearls, fine linen, purple cloth, silk, scarlet cloth, all kinds of scented wood, all kinds of articles of ivory, all kinds of articles of costly wood, bronze, iron and marble, cinnamon, spice, incense, myrrh, frankincense, wine, oil, fine flour, wheat, cattle and sheep, horses and chariots, and slaves, that is, human souls. "The fruit for which your soul longed has gone from you, and all your delicacies and your splendors are lost to you, never to be found again!" (Rv 18:11–14)

The luxuries and lusts of the world which can never fulfill human longing will, in a single hour, be burned up in a great conflagration mirroring the destruction of Sodom (Rv 18:10, 19). Like James warns, the rich will "weep and howl" for the miseries that will have come upon them (Jas 5:1). When the end of the world finally comes, it may be attended by widespread poverty, starvation, and riots, but I think it is more likely to come while much of the world is feasting, dancing, and enjoying the luxuries of this life.

In contrast to this carnal circus, we are told to watch and wait, so that that day does not surprise us like a thief. Do not sleep, as the world does, but keep awake and be sober. Those who sleep, sleep at night, and those who get drunk, are drunk at night. But though judgment is coming against all the worldliness of man, God has not destined us for wrath, but to obtain salvation through our Lord Jesus Christ (1 Thes 5:4–9). So keep awake. Be sober. And flee the carnival.

---

26   Etienne de la Boetie and Murray N. Rothbard, *The Politics of Obedience*, trans. Harry Kurtz (Auburn, Alabama: The Mises Institute, 1975), 65.

APOCALYPSE-PREPARATION LIST

- Resolve not to be spiritually compromised by entertainment and fleshly pursuits.
- For refreshment, practice creative, rather than consumptive practices.
- Give up comfort dependencies, including technology. Once you have learned to go without and are confident you *can* do it, cautiously decide what to use, and how to do so effectively and ethically.
- Give sacrificially of your money in order to free yourself from the hooks and barbs of material wealth.
- Fast from food and other enjoyments regularly to train your body and its desires.
- Practice contentment with little. Give thanks to God for food, clothing, and shelter, even if this is all you have, or may ever have.
- Memorize Matthew 6:19–24. "Do not lay up for yourselves treasures on earth, where moth and rust destroy and where thieves break in and steal, but lay up for yourselves treasures in heaven, where neither moth nor rust destroys and where thieves do not break in and steal. For where your treasure is, there your heart will be also. The eye is the lamp of the body. So, if your eye is healthy, your whole body will be full of light, but if your eye is bad, your whole body will be full of darkness. If then the light in you is darkness, how great is the darkness! No one can serve two masters, for either he will hate the one and love the other, or he will be devoted to the one and despise the other. You cannot serve God and money."

CHAPTER 3

Resist the Mind-Control

YOUR ATTENTION PLEASE!

Abraham Lincoln's momentous Peoria, Illinois speech on October 16, 1854, was a crucial step in the revitalization of his political career.[1] In the address, he articulated his opposition to slavery and to the recently passed Kansas-Nebraska Act. This act, championed by Democrat and regular sparring partner Stephen Douglas, repealed the earlier Missouri Compromise and threatened, according to Lincoln, to both tear apart the union and enshrine state rights to slavery. Douglas, at that point one of the most popular politicians in the United States, began the highly attended debate with a three-hour address. Lincoln's turn to respond came at the 5pm mark, and so he proposed that the audience go home for dinner and "return refreshed for four more hours of talk," to which they agreed.[2] Lincoln's speech upon their return that evening is still recognized as a persuasive masterpiece, and a significant turning point for the country in the eventual abolition of slavery.

As incredible as a seven-hour debate sounds, this was not unusual at the time. Referring to the Peoria debate in *Amusing Ourselves to Death*, Neil Postman asked in 1985, "Is there any audience of Americans today who could endure seven hours of talk? Or five or three? Especially without pictures of any kind?"[3] This slide in attention has only accelerated since.

---

1   James G. Randall, "Abraham Lincoln," in *Dictionary of American Biography, Vol. 6* (Charles Scribner's Sons, 1961), 247.

2   Neil Postman, *Amusing Ourselves to Death* (New York: Penguin, 2014), 44.

3   Postman, *Amusing Ourselves to Death*, 45.

To a new generation of always-connected consumers, the Internet has supplied a never-ending and mostly mindless drip of news headlines, social interaction, and video content. In 2016, Facebook marketing director Michelle Klein stated that the average adult checks their phone 30 times a day.[4] In contrast, the average millennial, she noted at the time, checks their phone more than 157 times per day.[5] Nothing interesting on your Twitter or Facebook feed one of those 157 times? Simply hit refresh! Constantly distracted, we have become incapable of sustained contemplation and deep thought.

Considered a pleasant pastime throughout the last few centuries, even reading has been severely impacted by modern distraction-culture. Author David Ulin relates an experience to which most readers can relate:

> These days, after spending hours on the computer, I pick up a book and read a paragraph; then my mind wanders and I check my e-mail, drift onto the Internet, pace the house before returning to the page. Or I want to do these things but don't, force myself to remain still, to follow what I'm reading until I give myself to the flow. What I'm struggling with is the encroachment of the buzz, the sense that there is something out there that merits my attention, when in fact it's mostly just a series of disconnected riffs, quick takes and fragments, that add up to the anxiety of the age.[6]

Nicholas Carr noticed this same effect in his own life and began exploring how the Internet transforms the minds of those who use it. The result was *The Shallows*, a book that traces the history of media and how it changes our brains. He chronicles how tools, whether the typewriter or the modern computer, transform not only our efficiency and output, but the very means by which we process information. Our brains are plastic—they are constantly changing at a neurological level as they adapt to activities and practices. "As particular circuits in our brain strengthen through the repetition of a physical or mental activity, they begin to transform that activity into a habit."[7] These habits could

---

4   Zuboff, *The Age of Surveillance Capitalism*, 448.
5   Zuboff, *The Age of Surveillance Capitalism*, 448.
6   David Ulin, *The Lost Art of Reading* (Seattle: Sasquatch Books, 2010), 35.
7   Nicholas Carr, *The Shallows* (New York: W. W. Nortoin & Co., 2010), 34.

be good or bad, but the deck seems particularly stacked these days against building good habits of the mind. The web's optimized and reactive algorithms are highly adept at transforming that quick check of messages into twenty minutes of diversion—Facebook and Google's bottom-lines require it. As Carr aphorizes, "Our use of the Internet involves many paradoxes, but the one that promises to have the greatest long-term influence over how we think is this one: the Net seizes our attention only to scatter it."[8]

Generations are being trained to meander meaninglessly through new-media drivel, attractively polished and packaged by tech companies in entertainment's best glitter and gloss. The depth and breadth of knowledge available online is astonishing, and yet fewer and fewer people seem capable of logical processing or rational debate. Everything is available, all at once, and usually wrapped up in bite-sized packages so that the consumer does not have to think much. Artificial intelligence indeed!

THE HIVE-MIND

At the same time as our "intelligence" is getting more and more synthetic, the artificial intelligence (AI) behind the Internet is transforming us into its image by the renewing of our minds. It is not merely that our attention is easily diverted away from accomplishing more useful activities. It is not only that our brains are being re-wired to disfavour thinking and meditation. Far more alarmingly in recent decades, technological platforms are actively seeking to *modify* behaviour to align with the philosophy and worldview of those behind the controls. It is the all-seeing, all-knowing, and increasingly powerful AI which allows them to accomplish their goals. As Eric Schmidt of Google stated already in 2010, "You give us more information about you, your friends, and we can improve the quality of our searches. We don't need you to type at all. We know where you are. We know where you've been. We

---

8   Carr, *The Shallows*, 118.

can more or less know what you are thinking about."[9]

We noted in the introduction how Google, Facebook, and other companies' extraction of personal data is a profit-driven freight-train. Shoshana Zuboff, however, notes that this no-holds-barred approach to financial gain has led to their seeking the holy grail of monetization, which is to control what the masses think and want. "The surest way to predict behaviour," she remarks, "is to intervene at its source and shape it."[10]

> These interventions are designed to enhance certainty by doing things: they nudge, herd, manipulate, and modify behavior in specific directions by executing actions as subtle as inserting a specific phrase into your Facebook news feed, timing the appearance of a BUY button on your phone, or shutting down your car engine when an insurance payment is late.[11]

When it comes to behavioral modification and manipulation, Facebook "is the crucible of this new dark science."[12] Over one thousand real-time experiments have been conducted by their data science group, experiments which clearly demonstrate their ability to manipulate emotion and outcomes.[13] As one example, Facebook teamed up in 2012 with researchers at Cornell University to conduct a study with a sample size of 689,003 unsuspecting participants, "possibly the largest in the history of psychology," proving the widespread effect of the manipulation of emotions on the platform.[14] The study provoked serious ethical concerns and when questions were asked of Susan T. Fiske, editor of the published study, why established ethical procedures were not followed, she argued that "Facebook manipulates people's feeds all the time"![15]

---

9   Zuboff, *The Age of Surveillance Capitalism*, 498.

10   Zuboff, *The Age of Surveillance Capitalism*, 200.

11   Zuboff, *The Age of Surveillance Capitalism*, 200.

12   Zuboff, *The Age of Surveillance Capitalism*, 468.

13   Zuboff, *The Age of Surveillance Capitalism*, 302.

14   Chris Chambers, "Facebook Fiasco: Was Cornell's Study of 'Emotional Contagion' an Ethics Breach?," *The Guardian*, July 1, 2014, https://www.theguardian.com/science/head-quarters/2014/jul/01/facebook-cornell-study-emotional-contagion-ethics-breach.

15   Zuboff, *The Age of Surveillance Capitalism*, 302.

Chillingly, Zuboff summarizes, "In declaring the right to modify human action secretly and for profit, surveillance capitalism effectively exiles us from our own behavior, shifting the locus of control over the future tense from 'I will' to 'You will.'"[16] Zuboff dubs this ubiquitous, AI-state "Big Other," however, it does not seem far away either from "the Borg," Star Trek's one-mind alien uber-enemy in *Star Trek: The Next Generation*. "Big Other does not care what we think, feel or do," elucidates Zuboff, "as long as its millions, billions, and trillions of sensate, actuating, computational eyes and ears can observe, render, datafy, and instrumentalize the vast reservoirs of behavioural surplus that are generated in the galactic uproar of connection and communication."[17] When faced with the staggering breadth and ubiquity of surveillance capitalism, not to mention what lies on the horizon, it can easily feel that resistance is futile.[18]

The ground-breaking work in *The Age of Surveillance Capitalism* paints a picture of a world careening towards a nightmarish techno-dystopia. In at least one aspect, however, the reality may be more pessimistic still. There is a more malevolent motivation than profit behind this technocratic trajectory. The scriptures describe a dark will pulling the strings of world-power— "the prince of the power of the air, the spirit that is now at work in the sons of disobedience" (Eph 2:2). It ought not to be surprising, therefore, that what mega-corporations desire, increasingly, is not just more cash, but a particular kind of society that matches their "progressive" and increasingly anti-Christ beliefs.

There are inordinate pressures upon you day after day to behave a certain way, to go with the flow, to move with the herd, to make your home with the rest of the hive. In order to resist and to exercise

---

16   Zuboff, *The Age of Surveillance Capitalism*, 308.

17   Zuboff, *The Age of Surveillance Capitalism*, 377.

18   "The result is that 'policies' are functionally equivalent to plans, as Big Other directs human and machine action. It ensures that doors will be locked or unlocked, car engines will shut down or come to life, the jackhammer will scream "no" in suicidal self-sacrifice, the workers will adhere to norms, the group will swarm to defeat anomalies. We will all be safe as each organism hums in harmony with every other organism, less a society than a population that ebbs and flows in perfect frictionless confluence, shaped by the means of behavioural modification that elude our awareness and thus can neither be mourned nor resisted" Zuboff, 410–11.

your God-given, Christ-renewed will, you will need to have a deeply transformed and gospel-saturated mind trained and responsive to God's word, rather than to the omniscient and omnipresent "we" of the emerging AI techno-state.

THE EXPERTS AND THE REPORTERS

One of the clearest examples of thought-control in Western culture is the left-wing capture of mainstream news media. Celebrated journalist Sharyl Attkisson laments the current state of journalism and its almost complete adherence to what she calls "The Narrative," the story that is being told in how news events are reported, framed, and even "fact-checked." A five-time Emmy award-winner and previous news anchor at both CNN and CBS, Attkisson chronicles the demise of true journalism in *Slanted*, including at newspapers as previously reputable as *The Washington Post* and *The New York Times*.

One noteworthy example was the *Washington Post's* October 2019 headline for its article on the death of ISIS leader Abu Bakr al-Baghdadi. Several years prior, I remember receiving reports as ISIS swept through the country of Iraq, and praying in church for Christian missionaries whose children were executed in front of them when they refused to denounce their faith in Jesus Christ. Particularly infamous were the many video-recorded beheadings perpetrated by ISIS, seen by millions around the world. For several years, Al-Baghdadi was the world's most-wanted man. He finally died in a night-raid by American forces when he detonated a suicide vest that not only killed him but also three of his children. In spite of the barbarity and heinousness of his life, the day after his death, the *Post's* headline read, "Abu Bakr al-Baghdadi, austere religious scholar at helm of Islamic State, dies at 48."[19] The shockingly anodyne headline provoked a social media firestorm. Twitter exploded with similarly positive death-notice parodies of Hitler, Genghis Khan, and others. Eventually, the *Post* changed

---

19   The first version of the headline read "Abu Bakr al-Bahdadi, Islamic State's 'Terrorist in Chief,' dies at 48." There were several iterations of the headline. Sharyl Attkisson, *Slanted* (New York: HarperCollins, 2020), 118.

the headline.

Islamic extremism seems to be a particularly thorny issue for mainstream media. Less than two months earlier, on the anniversary of 9/11, the *New York Times* published a tweet that stated, "18 years have passed since airplanes took aim and brought down the World Trade Center."[20] One would think it would be salient to name the perpetrators of the largest terrorist attack on North American soil in history, rather than attribute it to inanimate machines.

Bias is a feature of mainstream media on both the left and the right. People want to hear their viewpoints confirmed and a profitable niche can often be carved out doing precisely that. But the rise in popularity of centrist and right-wing media companies confirms that traditional media companies are increasingly losing the trust of the average citizen. For instance, not only does Fox News draw the largest percentage of conservative viewers among cable news networks, but it also draws the largest percentage of liberal viewers, more than eight percent more than its nearest rival, MSNBC![21] CNN in particular, has cratered in viewership, recently hitting seven-year lows.[22] Lou Waters, a onetime CNN anchor, states "I can't watch CNN," lamenting that factual news reporting on it and other networks has been replaced by opinion and expert panels.[23]

It was this reliance upon biased "experts" among mainstream media news networks that contributed to one of the most egregious examples of bias, corruption, and election interference in U.S. history—the suppression of the Hunter Biden laptop story. The *New York Post* broke the story only twenty-one days before the 2020 Presidential election. Hunter, the troubled son of then-presidential candidate Joe

---

20   Attkisson, 127.

21   Andy Meek, "Fox News Channel Has Now Spent 20 Years In The #1 Spot On The Cable News Rankings," *Forbes*, February 1, 2022, https://www.forbes.com/sites/andymeek/2022/02/01/fox-news-channel-has-now-spent-20-years-in-the-1-spot-on-the-cable-news-rankings/?sh=4373a0fd72f2.

22   Mark Joyella, "CNN's Ratings Woes Continue As Network Has Its Lowest-Rated Week In More Than 7 Years," *Forbes*, March 14, 2023, https://www.forbes.com/sites/markjoyella/2023/03/14/cnns-ratings-woes-continue-as-network-has-its-lowest-rated-week-in-more-than-7-years/?sh=2a6a369710a6.

23   Attkisson, *Slanted*, 192.

Biden, had left his laptop at a repair shop in Delaware, and its contents were explosive, including evidence of Hunter's use of drugs and prostitutes.[24] More damaging yet, however, were emails which indicated a pay-for-play scheme to the tune of millions of dollars, with at least one email possibly implicating Joe Biden himself as a beneficiary.[25]

The mass media's response was immediate as they circled the wagons around their favored candidate. *Politico* published an article with the headline "Hunter Biden Story is Russian Disinfo, Dozens of Former Intel Officials Say."[26] Former Director of National intelligence, James Clapper, went on CNN to state it was Russian disinformation.[27] Twitter prevented its users from sharing the *New York Post's* bombshell story and Facebook reduced the story's distribution across its ubiquitous platform.[28] For two weeks the *New York Post* was completely locked out of Twitter on account of the story until Twitter CEO Jack Dorsey was summoned by Congress to account for its censorship. [29]

Elon Musk's purchase of Twitter in late 2022 and his release of internal documents to journalists Matt Taibbi and Bari Weiss in December of that year, confirmed some of the worst suspicions about the company's biased practices. Taibbi's reporting, carried out on the Twitter platform, substantiated the suppression of the Hunter Biden story and that the Twitter censors had responded to personal requests by Joe Biden's team about articles that ought to be dealt with.[30] Six days later, Weiss chronicled the regular blacklisting and content suppression of

---

24   Hemingway, *Rigged*, 240–41.

25   Hemingway, *Rigged*, 241.

26   Natasha Bertrand, "Hunter Biden Story Is Russian Disinfo, Dozens of Former Intel Officials Say," *Politico*, October 19, 2020, https://www.politico.com/news/2020/10/19/hunter-biden-story-russian-disinfo-430276.

27   Post Editorial Board, "Spies Who Lie: 51 'Intelligence' Experts Refuse to Apologize for Discrediting True Hunter Biden Story," *New York Post*, March 18, 2022, https://nypost.com/2022/03/18/intelligence-experts-refuse-to-apologize-for-smearing-hunter-biden-story/.

28   Hemingway, *Rigged*, 243.

29   Hemingway, *Rigged*, 243.

30   "By 2020, requests from connected actors to delete tweets were routine. One executive would write to another: 'More to review from the Biden team.' The reply would come back: 'Handled.'" Jordan Boyd, "'Twitter Files' Confirm Big Tech Leftists Suppressed Hunter Biden Laptop Story Ahead Of 2020 Election," *The Federalist*, December 3, 2022, https://thefederalist.com/2022/12/03/twitter-files-confirm-big-tech-leftists-suppressed-hunter-biden-laptop-story-ahead-of-2020-election/.

prominent conservatives on the platform—in direct contradiction to Twitter's public claims otherwise.[31]

On March 17, 2022, many months after the election, the *New York Times* finally admitted that the contents of the laptop were authentic. But as Pulitzer-Prize winning journalist Glenn Greenwald, who was himself censored over the story, points out, the ability to verify the story using accepted journalistic practices was there from the very beginning.[32] In fact, as reporter Mollie Hemmingway writes in *Rigged*, Tony Bobulinski, one of Hunter Biden's partners in his deal with the Chinese businessman in question, Ye Jianming, was willing to go on record with the *Wall Street Journal* that Biden knew about the deal, was willing to profit from it, and that he had met Joe Biden personally to discuss the matter. The *Wall Street Journal* refused to print it.[33]

The suppression of the Hunter Biden story just prior to the 2020 election, with its implication of President Joe Biden in foreign corruption, may go down as one of the most egregious examples of election interference in US history. Mainstream media outlets colluded with corrupt "experts" to spread misinformation and suppress truthful reporting to make certain that the Democrats did not lose to Donald Trump a second time.

TRUST THE SCIENCE

No one expects experts to be infallible. Shifting contexts and new data may impact an authority's ability to provide information that stands the test of time. Recently, however, there seems to be a troubling juxtaposition: expert opinion is increasingly portrayed as inscrutable and inerrant, while at the same time many of these pundits are succumbing to

---

31   "In 2018, Twitter's head of legal policy and trust Vijaya Gadde (since fired by Musk) and head of product Kayvon Beykpour stated: 'We do not shadow ban.... And we certainly don't shadow ban based on political viewpoints or ideology.'" Ari Blaff, "Twitter Suppressed Prominent Right-Wing, Anti-Lockdown Users Documents Show," *National Review*, December 8, 2022, https://www.nationalreview.com/news/twitter-suppressed-prominent-right-wing-anti-lockdown-users-documents-show/.

32   Lindsay Kornick, "Glenn Greenwald Rips Washington Post Verifying Hunter Biden Laptop: 'Now When It's Safe to Say It,'" *Fox News*, March 30, 2022, foxnews.com/media/glenn-greenwald-wapo-hunter-report.

33   Hemmingway, *Rigged*, 244.

corruption, bias, and in some cases, outright lies. Consider this—in the inexorable march of scientific progress, we have finally arrived at the place where we no longer know what a man or a woman is![34] This is in spite of the fact that every human being is a product of sexual union.[35]

My involvement in advocacy around gender and transgender issues over the last number of years has alerted me to the tremendous amount of bias in the medical field—a domain one might reasonably assume to be among the purest of disciplines. For instance, arguably the three most renowned sexologists of the last couple decades—Ray Blanchard, Michael Bailey, and Ken Zucker—oppose the affirmation-only paradigm for treating gender dysphoria which has now almost completely overtaken medical and psychological practice in North America.[36] Anyone who reads the sexology literature knows these names are unquestioned leaders in the field. And yet each of them has been sidelined and attacked in a variety of ways in order to portray their opinions as fringe, or even dangerous. Although inquiries, where they have occurred, have vindicated them,[37] their ostracization from influence in those fields in which they are leaders permits medical organizations and legislators to speak of a scientific consensus on transgender issues when in reality, the leading experts are against the so-called "consensus." In this climate of cancel culture and institutional capture, the mantra, "trust the experts," ends up meaning "trust the experts the mainstream narrative tells you to trust."

I have seen some of the same tactics regarding COVID, vaccines, lockdowns, and mandates, in which honest debate has been

---

34   Caroline Downey, "Judge Jackson Refuses to Define 'Woman' during Confirmation Hearing: 'I'm Not a Biologist'," *National Review*, March 23, 2022, nationalreview.com/news/judge-jackson-refuses-to-define-woman-during-confirmation-hearing-im-not-a-biologist.

35   Or at the very least, the union of sexually dimorphic gametes.

36   J. Michael Bailey and Ray Blanchard, "Gender Dysphoria Is Not One Thing," *4thWaveNow*, 2017, https://4thwavenow.com/2017/12/07/gender-dysphoria-is-not-one-thing/; Kenneth J. Zucker, "The Myth of Persistence," *International Journal of Transgenderism* 19, no. 2 (2018): 231–45.

37   Molly Hayes, "Doctor Fired from Gender Identity Clinic Says He Feels 'Vindicated' after CAMH Apology, Settlement," *Globe and Mail*, October 7, 2018, theglobeandmail.com/canada/toronto/article-doctor-fired-from-gender-identity-clinic-says-he-feels-vindicated; Benedict Carey, "Criticism of a Gender Theory, and a Scientist Under Siege," *New York Times*, August 21, 2007, nytimes.com/2007/08/21/health/psychology/21gender.html.

silenced and the masses have somewhat blindly followed the establishment medical experts, even when their track record is demonstrably poor. For instance, an August 2021 CDC media statement promoted a study which seemed to indicate that vaccines provided better protection against COVID than natural immunity;[38] a January 2022 CDC study reported the opposite, stating that prior infection offers superior protection.[39] Regarding the question of the vaccinated possibly transmitting COVID, Dr. Anthony Fauci stated on May 16, 2021 that "vaccinated people become a dead end for the coronavirus;"[40] it is now abundantly clear that the vaccinated are able to transmit the virus.[41] On top of this are the revelations of Dr. Fauci's connections to gain-of-function virology research[42] and questions about a recent and significant rise in worldwide excess mortality of unknown cause which casts doubt on the worldwide COVID strategy which was pursued at the behest of the experts.[43] Is it any wonder that significant numbers of people are cautious when it comes to blindly "trusting the science?"

---

38   CDC, "New CDC Study: Vaccination Offers Higher Protection than Previous COVID-19 Infection," *Centers for Disease Control and Prevention*, 2021, https://www.cdc.gov/media/releases/2021/s0806-vaccination-protection.html.

39   Tomas et. al Leon, "COVID-19 Cases and Hospitalizations by COVID-19 Vaccination Status and Previous COVID-19 Diagnosis," *Centers for Disease Control and Prevention*, 2022, https://www.cdc.gov/mmwr/volumes/71/wr/mm7104e1.htm. The authors argue that this finding represents an actual change in vaccine effectiveness across strains, i.e. that vaccines offered more protection than natural infection in earlier, but not later strains. Even if this conclusion is correct, there is the irony that the strains mutate so fast that the experts were wrong about superior vaccine protection almost as soon as their advice was released. Gazit et al., however, suggest a possible methodological flaw in the earlier study which suggested greater protection for vaccines (p550). Sivan Gazit et al., "Severe Acute Respiratory Syndrome Coronavirus 2 (SARS-CoV-2) Naturally Acquired Immunity versus Vaccine-Induced Immunity , Reinfections versus Breakthrough Infections : A Retrospective Cohort Study," *Clinical Infectious Diseases* 75, no. 1 (2022): e545–51, https://doi.org/https://doi.org/10.1093/cid/ciac262.

40   Joseph Choi, "Fauci: Vaccinated People Become 'Dead Ends' for the Coronavirus," *The Hill*, May 16, 2021, https://thehill.com/homenews/sunday-talk-shows/553773-fauci-vaccinated-people-become-dead-ends-for-the-coronavirus/?rl=1.

41   Iivo Hetemäki et al., "An Outbreak Caused by the SARS-CoV-2 Delta Variant (B . 1 . 617 . 2) in a Secondary Care Hospital in Finland, May 2021," *Eurosurveillance* 26, no. 30 (2021): 1–6, https://doi.org/10.2807/1560-7917.ES.2021.26.30.2100636.

42   See chapter 7.

43   Ross Clark, "What's to Blame for the Surge in Excess Deaths?," *The Spectator*, August 19, 2022, spectator.co.uk/article/what-s-to-blame-for-the-surge-in-excess-deaths.

Whether in reference to scientific or cultural matters, personal health or politics, the Christian must recognize the warfare being waged against the reasoning faculties of his mind and, as Francis Schaeffer stated decades ago, not to "uncritically accept what they read, and especially what they see on television, as objective."[44] Although this chapter is not about COVID or the medical industry, the news or the Internet, it is about how you are being pressured and told what to think.

NEW MIND

Your mind is under constant bombardment. This is not by accident. It is a strategic assault by the forces of evil, in the knowledge that the mind is what John Calvin called the "citadel" to the soul,[45] the pre-eminent part of man set by his Creator to be the control hub for his entire life. Infiltrate the mind, therefore, and you subvert the whole man. In an important sense, we are actually born subverted because original sin has infected the mind. This is why the new creation that is through faith in Jesus Christ is so often presented in Scripture as a transformation of mind and a right relationship to truth. Those without this renewal are "alienated and hostile in mind" (Col 1:21). They live not only in the evil desires of the flesh but also those of the mind (Eph 2:3). "To the defiled and unbelieving, nothing is pure; but both their minds and their consciences are defiled" (Ti 1:15).

The Christian, however, must not be conformed to the thinking of this world, but is instead to be transformed by the renewal of his mind, so that by testing he may discern the will of God, what is good and acceptable and perfect (Rom 12:2). We are to set our minds not on the things of the flesh, but on things of the Holy Spirit (Rom 8:6–7). It is by this Spirit that we are enabled to judge all things, for through Him and His regeneration we are given the mind of Christ (1 Cor 2:14–16).

---

44   Francis A. Schaeffer, "The Christian Manifesto," in *The Complete Works of Francis A. Shaeffer* (Westchester, Il: Crossway Books, 1982), 450.

45   Obbie Tyler Todd, "The Preeminence of Knowledge in John Calvin's Doctrine of Conversion and Its Influence upon His Ministry in Geneva," *Themelios* 42, no. 2 (2017): 312.

It is only an intellect set free by the truth of Christ which will be able to withstand the onslaught of the foretold deceptiveness of the last days. Paul warns in 2 Thessalonians 2:9–12 that

> The coming of the lawless one is by the activity of Satan with all power and false signs and wonders, and with all wicked deception for those who are perishing, because they refused to love the truth and so be saved. Therefore God sends them a strong delusion, so that they may believe what is false, in order that all may be condemned who did not believe the truth but had pleasure in unrighteousness.

The Lord Jesus, in fact, stated that "false christs and false prophets will arise and perform great signs and wonders, so to lead astray, if possible, even the elect" (Mt 24:24).

More than ever, the church of Jesus Christ must be committed to the life of the mind, and to a robust and distinctly Christian view of philosophy, science, arts, politics, and education. Pastors need to preach to the mind, and through the mind to wills and hearts, as seen in the approaches of John Calvin and Jonathan Edwards.[46] We need polemical and apologetic teaching carried out in the right spirit. If we are not able to show the intellectual bankruptcy of the world's thinking; if we cannot unveil the deception and biases inherent in mainstream media; if we refuse to build a firm educational foundation able to withstand the gusty gales of "every wind of doctrine" (Eph 4:14), the church's decline will only accelerate and we will continue to lose generations of our children to the Beast's system, especially as represented in higher education.

STATE OF EDUCATION

In Christian circles it has become well known, and to many intensely and grievously personal, that the church is losing its young people to the world, and especially to secular universities. Research by the Barna Group indicates that 64% of American Christian young people leave the church in young adulthood, and the percentage is almost identical

---

46   Todd, "The Preeminence of Knowledge."

among young Canadian Evangelicals according to the Evangelical Fellowship of Canada's *Hemorrhaging Faith* report.[47] Researchers have suggested several reasons for this exodus, and I will argue in the next chapter that a lack of intentional family discipleship may explain much of the waywardness of our children. But it is clear that the hostility of secular colleges and universities is the context in which the lack of a resilient and mature faith is revealed in many of these church-raised students.

In *The Parasitic Mind*, Canadian university professor Gad Saad notes the incredible one-sidedness of the worldviews of university professors.

> In a 2016 study of professors' voting registration at forty leading American universities across five disciplines, the Democrat-to-Republican ratios were 4.5 (economics), 33.5 (history), 20.0 (journalism), 8.6 (law), and 17.4 (psychology). The total across the five disciplines was an 11.5 to 1 ratio favoring Democratic professors.[48]

I can think of left-leaning professors from whose experience I would want to glean. But an eleven to one ratio? Our universities and colleges are not so much places of higher education as they are liberal indoctrination centres. Progressives have strategically conquered post-secondary educational institutions and they now churn out secularist advocates convinced, either via persuasion or pressure, that abortion is a human right, historic Western thought is evil, and that society must be tolerant of everything except for objective morality.

Public elementary and high schools may be slightly less hostile to Christian thought, but not by much. Socialism is openly lauded. Critical Race Theory enforces victim-culture. And here in Canada, pagan rituals associated with First Nations religious practices are foist-

---

47   David Kinnaman, "Church Dropouts Have Risen to 64%—But What About Those Who Stay?," *Barna Group*, 2019, https://www.barna.com/research/resilient-disciples/; James Penner et al., "Hemorrhaging Faith: Why and When Canadian Young Adults Are Leaving, Staying and Returning to Church," 2011, https://hemorrhaging-faith.com/.

48   Gad Saad, *The Parastic Mind* (Washington, DC: Regnery Publishing, 2021), 63. The study referenced is Mitchell Langbert, Anthony J. Quain, and Daniel B. Klein, "Faculty Voter Registration in Economics, History, Journalism, Law, and Psychology," *Econ Journal Watch* 13, no. 3 (2016): 422–51.

ed on young children, forcing them and their parents to "opt out."[49] At least currently, parents *are* permitted to withdraw their children from these pagan ceremonies. When it comes to gender theories which are taught starting in Kindergarten, there is no opting out in many locales.[50]

In spite of some excellent teachers and even some good school districts, this widening program of cultural conditioning is, at its root, an anti-Christ, humanistic religious endeavour. As Joe Boot states, "In order to 'save' people from themselves and their ignorance, the state and its educational apparatus becomes the new redeeming order; the classroom is the new pulpit, the curriculum the new bible, and the state educators the new priesthood."[51]

Many parents are unsurprisingly finding alternatives to state education. Unlike many places in Europe, homeschooling is a legal option in Canada and the United States. According to a recent study in the United States, homeschooling rates hovered for over ten years around 3.3% up until 2012 when they began to slowly rise.[52] However, COVID and its educational repercussions created a spark of sudden interest in homeschooling which has since exploded. In 2021, the percentage of US households homeschooling their children more than doubled, rising from 5.4% to 11.1%.[53] I hear regularly not only from Conservatives but self-proclaimed Liberals and Leftists who are considering homeschooling because of the failures of the public school system, both ideologically and academically.

The challenge for many families is the cost associated with non-public schooling. Modern Western economies are built upon the assumption of a two-income family, and nowhere is that truer than in my place of residence, Greater Vancouver, BC, one of the most expen-

---

49   In April 2022, a blessing of the Skwo:wech Elementary School in New Westminster, BC included a smudging ceremony.

50   I have heard countless personal stories both by teachers and parents about mandatory SOGI lessons here in BC, Canada.

51   Joe Boot, *The Mission of God*, 2nd Edition (Toronto: Ezra Press, 2016), 432.

52   Casey Eggleston and Jason Fields, "Census Bureau's Household Pulse Survey Shows Significant Increase in Homsechooling Rates in Fall 2020," *United States Census Bureau*, March 22, 2021, https://www.census.gov/library/stories/2021/03/homeschooling-on-the-rise-during-covid-19-pandemic.html.

53   Eggleston and Fields.

sive places to live in the world, relative to income.[54] For many families, especially immigrant families working hard to start new lives here, homeschooling represents an enormous, perhaps even seemingly impossible financial sacrifice. Private Christian schools are another alternative, but they are costly and many of them are succumbing to anti-scriptural worldviews as they are pressured by the world and governments to which they are often linked financially. In chapter 5, I will argue that we are in desperate need of pioneering new educational institutions and paradigms to address these concerns. But the solution starts with Christian parents who are willing to make sacrifices and take seriously God's command that they, and not the state, have been given the responsibility to teach their children. Education—which is nothing less than the total life governed by the mind—starts in the home, and with holy habits.

HOLY HABITS

In order to bolster the life of the spiritually renewed intellect, God has enjoined us to practices that renew the mind with Scripture, especially meditation and memorization. As the prophet Isaiah proclaims, "To the teaching and to the testimony!" (Is 8:20).

Scriptural meditation is the practice of thinking deeply about God's Word with a view to internalize and apply its truths. In the foreword to David Saxton's book *God's Battle Plan for the Mind*, Joel Beeke illustrates the practice of meditation by way of an illustration.

> Imagine being invited to a private dinner hosted by a friend who works as a chef in a five-star restaurant. This person is renowned for cooking meals that are nutritious, healthy, delightful, and satisfying. You can hardly wait for the day to arrive. Finally it comes, and from the moment you step in the front door, you are embraced by tantalizing aromas. As the host seats you, the colors and arrangement of the food on various dishes are a feast for the eyes. Your friend has thoughtfully chosen your favorite foods. However, just as you sink your fork into the first bite and raise it to your lips, your phone chirps

---

54   "Demographia International Housing Affordability: 2022 Edition," 2022, http://demographia.com/dhi.pdf.

like a cuckoo clock gone mad. The strident voice on the line is your boss's, and before he finishes his first sentence you know that you will never eat the delicacies set before you. With a rumbling stomach and a tight smile, you make your excuses and head out the door. You saw the food and smelled it, but never chewed it, digested it, or benefited from it. That is the Christian life without meditation.[55]

Meditation on God's Word is what fuels the fire of our heart's love for Christ and His will. Reading involves the sensory process of scanning written text and the cognitive process of discerning its meaning. But even the best literature, even *Spirit-inspired* literature, is useless for the heart and life unless it steeps and stews in us. The Puritan writer Thomas Watson elucidated,

> Meditation without reading is erroneous; reading without meditation is barren. The bee sucks the flower and then works it into the hive, and so turns it into honey. By reading we suck the flower of the Word, by meditation we work it into the hive of our mind, and so it turns to profit.... The reason we come away so cold from the reading of the Word is because we do not warm ourselves at the fire of meditation.[56]

As we have considered, the world wants to scatter your attention and keep you from sustained contemplation about God and His world. Educator Charlotte Mason states, "no intellectual habit is so valuable as that of attention."[57] If the devil cannot keep you from reading the Bible, he will do the next best thing and keep you from sitting undisturbed in some quiet place in order to meditate. The distraction may be via some flittering thought— "what about that email I sent last night?" It may be via some physical reflex—a reaching for the cellphone to see the latest news or feed. Or it may be that the work and trouble of the day comes crashing in to disturb your thoughts. But a renewed, focused, and precise mind is developed by stillness and meditating on knowing God (Ps 46:10). We prepare our minds for action by

---

55   David W. Saxton, *God's Battle Plan for the Mind: The Puritan Practice of Biblical Meditation* (Grand Rapids, MI: Reformation Heritage Books, 2015).

56   Saxton, Kindle Loc. 1390.

57   Charlotte Mason, "Three Instruments of Education," in *Towards a Philosophy of Education* (Radford, VA: Wilder Publications, 2008), 80.

setting our hope *fully* on the future grace we will receive in Christ (1 Pt 1:13).

Memorization is another crucial habit to protect and renew our minds. The human mind is capable of great feats of memory, but our entertainment-driven media culture has largely obliterated our ability to retain what we read or memorize. As Nicholas Carr reminds us, however, we can retrain and strengthen our minds and memories.

> We don't constrain our mental powers when we store new long-term memories. We strengthen them. With each expansion of our memory comes an enlargement of our intelligence. The Web provides a convenient and compelling supplement to personal memory, but when we start using the Web as a substitute for personal memory, bypassing the inner processes of [memory] consolidation, we risk emptying our minds of their riches.[58]

Our greatest riches are those of God's Word. We are instructed to treasure up the Lord's commandments within ourselves (Prv 2:1). They will shield us, guard our path in justice, and watch over our way (Prv 2:7–8). They will deliver us from men who speak lies, from those who delight in evil, and from temptresses who offer forbidden pleasures (Prv 2:12–16).

It is tempting to be awed and overwhelmed by the memorization capabilities of past generations. According to Pliny the Elder, Lucius Scipio could name all the citizens of Rome.[59] The early church would not admit anyone into church office that did not have the Psalms memorized.[60] More recently, while imprisoned in a Russian Communist labor camp, Aleksandr Solzhenitsyn would write what would become *One Day in the Life of Ivan Denisovich* on scraps of paper, commit each scrap to memory, and then destroy it.[61]

However, as Carr suggests, the mind can be trained to increase its capacity no matter its current capability. Children in particular are

---

58   Carr, *The Shallows*, 192.

59   Pliny the Elder, *Natural History*, 7.24. It is, of course, possible that Scipio's prodigious memory was exaggerated by Pliny.

60   H. D. M. Spence-Jones, *Psalms, Vol. 1* (London; New York: Funk & Wagnalls, 1909), xii.

61   Lev Grossman, "Remembering Aleksandr Solzhenitsyn," *Time*, August 2008, http://content.time.com/time/arts/article/0,8599,1829150,00.html.

little sponges. Their ability, if it will be harnessed and improved, is such that entire books of the Bible could be reasonably memorized in childhood, serving to guard and strengthen them the rest of their lives. My mother began to memorize Scripture as a little girl. By memorizing a hundred verses she was awarded with a scholarship to go to summer camp. To this day she has many Epistles memorized, and a significant portion of the Psalms, including Psalm 119!

Even for adults without experience in memorization, much can be retained by the recitation of Scripture. Fifteen minutes per day of reading the Bible out loud could result in significant portions of Scripture being retained almost without trying. Sad to say that I am not as faithful as my mother when it comes to memorization. But our family regularly devotes a short portion of time after breakfast to memorizing and reciting Scripture, and our children now have multiple Psalms and chapters memorized, including the book of James. If we are going to send our children out into a hostile, indoctrinating world, they will need to have their souls and spirits armed and ready for that battle.

You are living in a world in which the Beast wants to control not only what you do, but what you think. And the scriptures warn us there is a day of widespread deception coming, sooner or later. Peter tells us to prepare our minds for action and to be self-controlled (1 Pt 1:13). So pay attention. Cultivate holy habits that renew the mind. Question everything taught by the world. Be alert to the dangers of modern technology. Resistance is not futile; it is both mandatory and possible. Resist the mind-control.

Apocalypse-Preparation List

- Minimize fast-moving media, especially social media.
- Read books. Not just news, social media, or internet articles—actual books.
- Don't implicitly trust the mainstream media or the so-called "experts." Be ready to do your own research. Look for those with a track-record of faithfulness and truth.
- Exit the public school system and make whatever sacrifices necessary to either home-school or enroll your children in a robustly Christian school so that they learn how to think.
- Meditate on God's word. Take a Scriptural thought and let it percolate undisturbed in your mind.
- Develop a program of memorizing Scripture. Give at least 10 minutes a day to memorizing and reciting.
- Memorize Psalm 19. "The heavens declare the glory of God, and the sky above proclaims his handiwork. Day to day pours out speech, and night to night reveals knowledge. There is no speech, nor are there words, whose voice is not heard. Their voice goes out through all the earth, and their words to the end of the world. In them he has set a tent for the sun, which comes out like a bridegroom leaving his chamber, and, like a strong man, runs its course with joy. Its rising is from the end of the heavens, and its circuit to the end of them, and there is nothing hidden from its heat. The law of the LORD is perfect, reviving the soul; the testimony of the LORD is sure, making wise the simple; the precepts of the LORD are right, rejoicing the heart; the commandment of the LORD is pure, enlightening the eyes; the fear of the LORD is clean, enduring forever; the rules of the LORD are true, and righteous altogether. More to be desired are they than gold, even much fine gold; sweeter also than honey and drippings of the honeycomb. Moreover, by them is your servant warned; in keeping them there is great reward. Who can discern his errors? Declare me innocent from hidden faults. Keep back your servant also from presumptuous sins; let them not have dominion over me! Then I shall be blameless, and innocent of great transgression. Let the words of my mouth and the meditation of my heart be acceptable in your sight, O LORD, my rock and my redeemer."

CHAPTER 4

Do Your Home-Work

THE FOUNDATION OF THE WORLD

In the Newberry-honored children's book, *Ella Enchanted*, the titular
character visits the land of the giants and is a guest at one of their weddings with its unique cultural trappings. The ceremony takes place in
a field and the couple enters holding hands, the bride carrying a sack,
and the groom a hoe. Both are clothed in trousers and a white smock.
Ella narrates that they

> began to plant a row of corn. He prepared the ground, and she
> dropped in seeds from her sack and covered them with moist earth.
> As they finished, clouds rolled in and a gentle rain fell, although the
> sky had been clear when the ceremony started. The giants spread their
> arms and tilted their heads to receive the drops.... The giants panto-
> mimed their lives together. They farmed and built a house and brought
> a series of older and older children from the audience into the imag-
> inary home, and then more babies for grandchildren. It ended when
> they lay down in the grass to signify their deaths together. Then they
> sprang up. Benches were overturned as giants poured onto the field to
> hug them and exclaim over the ceremony.[1]

Whether or not this fantasy wedding represents a societal ideal
for the author, Gail Carson Levine paints a beautiful and powerful picture. As strange as it would be, I cannot help but think that if weddings
all incorporated a life-pantomime, we would have a much healthier
society.

---

[1]   Gail Carson Levine, *Ella Enchanted*, Kindle (New York: HarperCollins,
1997), 121–22.

Throughout most of human history it has been a societal expectation that individuals would marry and have children (and grandchildren, if they lived long enough), before they died and left their offspring to continue their legacy. Personal identity was wrapped up in family identity—the life of the tribe and the clan.

This understanding of the family, and one's personal responsibility within it, is currently under attack. Some of the assailment is an artillery barrage, nonstop bombardment of sexual images and pornography in television and online media. Some of it is chemical warfare, cultural pressures arrayed against traditional sexual morality, seeping as it were into the fissures and cracks of our family loyalties. Some of it is brutal guerilla warfare, educators turning children against parents and their "bigoted" views on gender and sexuality. And some of it is Cold War-style propaganda, subtle messaging from an all-pervasive state, communicating that it is the child's true father and mother.

We will explore several of these contemporary strategies and tactics in this chapter. The warfare itself, however, is as old as the world. The Fall, for instance, describes not only the fall of man into sin, but the overthrow of the family as the serpent undermined Adam's authority, the first man failed to protect his wife, and the children born ever-after were born into sin and the strife it often brings, as seen in the account of Cain and Abel. God's response, thankfully, was that the family would not fail. In fact, redemption would be through one born of the very woman who first tasted sin (Gn 3:15). Ever since, the Dragon has been attacking the godly seed. Whether subtly, as when Abraham and Isaac failed to defend their wives from Beastly tyrants, or overtly, as when Leviathan-like Pharoah swallowed the Hebrew boys by casting them into the Nile, Satan has been trying to prevent his foretold doom at the hands of the promised one. These accounts are firstly to be understood as a preventative strike by the Devil against the Christ who would eventually come from Eve. They evidence too, however, that the enemy knows how fundamental the family is to the health and welfare of the world.

In the first chapter we remarked upon the dominion mandate of Genesis 1:27 which commands the extension of God's kingdom through struggle. To this we now add that this first law is framed within a particular context which presupposes that the family is the vehicle through which this dominion growth will take place—they are to "multiply and fill the earth." The family is fundamental to the kingdom and this truth is inherent in how male and female differently image God for the sake of procreation and discipleship.

The question of what constitutes the image of God has been hotly debated by theologians throughout church history.[2] Without entering into the broader debate, suffice to say that the context of Genesis 1 and 2 argues strongly that the capacity for relationships and family form at least part of that image.[3] The spread of the glory of God in the earth through the disciple-making process has always been dependent upon procreation. The importance of this insight for the life and mission of the church cannot be overstated. It means that the Lord's primary means of the extension of His kingdom is through faithful families raising godly children. Malachi 2:15 states about husband and wife, "Did he not make them one, with a portion of the Spirit in their union? And what was the one God seeking? Godly offspring."

Given the foundational importance of the family in Scripture, it is unsurprising that it is the focus of the Dragon's attack upon our world. The good news, however, is that God has endowed this institution with built-in power and resilience. If we do what we ought, God can and will not only protect our families in days of turmoil and tribulation, but will use them to bring about great glory and perhaps even revival.

Definitions Matter

Although the family has always been under attack, one of the most cunning and damaging offensives ever has recently been launched

---

2   For an overview, see Steve W. Lemke, "The Intelligent Design of Humans: The Meaning of the Imago Dei for Theological Anthropology," *Meeting of the Southwest Regional Evangelical Theological Society*, 2008, 12.

3   For the Trinitarian foundation for this, see J. Scott Horrell, "Toward a Biblical Model of the Social Trinity: Avoiding Equivocation of Nature and Order," *JETS* 47, no. 3 (2004): 399–421.

DEEP DISCIPLESHIP FOR DARK DAYS

against it, the undermining of the notion of "family" altogether. Until recently it has been an axiom, and accepted as self-evident, that marriage was for the purpose of procreation—to create families. In fact, the world's best philosophers and thinkers on marriage have recognized that the only way to ultimately define the institution is by grounding it upon ontological facts about mankind, namely upon personhood itself.

Plato is one example. In his *Laws*, his last dialogue, he states that the very first law of the state must accord with the first law of nature—namely that of generation. On account of generation coming from "the union and partnership of marriage," marriage must be any government's first law.[4] Notice the clarity of thinking here: marriage ought to exist because persons exist. The societal protection of marriage is primarily concerned with the fruit of that marriage. Anthropologist Edward Westermarck likewise summarizes in his chapter "The Origins of Marriage" in his three-volume opus *The History of Human Marriage*, "it appears that marriage and the family are most intimately connected with one another: it is originally for the benefit of the young that male and female continue to live together. We may therefore say that marriage is rooted in the family rather than the family in marriage."[5]

Christian theologians have pointed to this reality as well. Canadian philosopher Edward Tingley states, "Everyone alive comes from unions between one man and one woman... marriage is that form of male-female relationship that for millennia has seemed best for the creation of families."[6] Martin Luther, whose writings on marriage ever after reformed the institution, likewise emphasized, "marriage is the first and chief thing; for it is the beginning and origin of the whole life."[7]

---

4   Plato, *Laws*, I. 721a.

5   Edward Westermarck, "The Origins of Marriage," in *The History of Human Marriage, Vol. 1*, 5th ed. (New York, NY: Johnson Reprint, 1971), 72.

6   Edward Tingley, "Question 1 | Does a Right to Same-Sex Marriage Mean the Redefinition of Marriage?," *Held to the Light*, n.d.

7   Martin Luther, *Luther's Works, Vol. 5*, ed. Pelikan Jaroslav, Hilton Oswald, and Helmut Lehmann (Saint Louis: Concordia Publishing House, 1999), 188–89. "President Clinton's Defense of Marriage Act (1996) similarly states, 'At bottom, civil

Recently, there has been a lack of clarity in the church on this point. Denominations and Christian organizations have often failed to state that procreation is a definitive part of marriage. Marriage ought to be many things—exclusive and permanent among them. But it is the procreative nature inherent in heterosexual coupling that is marriage's defining characteristic.[8] Overlooking this truth is a small but fundamental error which sadly issues from the same cultural assumptions which lead some Christians to condone gay marriage as a right in a secular society—that marriage is a private good based on love.

The gay marriage mantra "love is love" is nonsensical from a legislative viewpoint. But it was politically successful. And it was successful not only in the legalization of gay marriage, but in destroying the idea and rights of the family. Make no mistake, the legalization of gay marriage constitutes an insidious attack upon traditional marriage. The two ideas cannot peacefully coexist; they are fundamentally opposed, and we are currently witnessing the defeat of the family as an idea and institution in Western society at the hands of the ideology behind gay marriage. Ontario's "All Families Are Equal Act" is one example. In the 2016 legislation, the words "father" and "mother" were removed and parenthood was defined as a contractual relationship of up to four adult "parents."[9] As the Association for Reformed Political Action (ARPA) states, "if the state can redefine the family and offer more 'options' or 'rights' by knocking family law off its foundations of marriage and blood relations, it can also take rights away.[10] What will become of parental rights if a 'family' is whatever the state says it is and a 'parent' is whoever the state says is a parent?"[11]

society has an interest in maintaining and protecting the institution of heterosexual marriage because it has a deep and abiding interesting in encouraging responsible procreation and child-rearing. Simply put, government has an interest in marriage because it has an interest in children.'" Cited from Katy Faust and Stacy Manning, *Them Before Us* (New York: Post Hill Press, 2021), 75.

8   For a helpful defense of the traditional definition of marriage, see Sherif Girgis, Ryan T. Anderson, and Robert P. George, *What Is Marriage? : Man and Woman : A Defense* (New York: Encounter Books, 2012).

9   Faust and Manning, *Them Before Us*, 78; "FAQ on Ontario's Bill 28, the 'All Families Are Equal Act,'" *ARPA Canada*, November 10, 2016, https://arpacanada.ca/articles/faq-ontarios-bill-28-families-equal-act/.

10   "FAQ on Ontario's Bill 28, the 'All Families Are Equal Act.'"

11   In 2018, a ruling by a Newfoundland and Labrador court in Canada "recog-

Children's rights activist Katy Faust lists other recent developments: "In 2018," she writes, "I witnessed the sponsor of Washington State's child-commodifying Uniform Parentage Act reason that laws recognizing mothers and fathers were unconstitutional, considering gay marriage was now the law of the land."[12] And in 2019, "The state of Virginia passed House Bill 1979 legalizing surrogacy, listing embryos as items that could be *owned* (the first time since 1860 that Virginia law designated a group of people as property), and scrubbing the words 'mother' and 'father' from parenthood law.[13]

SINS OF SELF-IDENTITY

Likening family to a contract or a commercial transaction undermines the intrinsic right parents have to their children. But the removal of parental rights isn't just a future nightmare. It has already begun, and it often centers on issues of sexual orientation and gender identity (SOGI).

In my work on the topic of SOGI, several parents have reported to me that their children were disturbed by sexualized teaching in the classroom, but when they followed up with the teacher or administrator, they were told that they were not entitled to know what their child was learning. In Alberta, a Gay-Straight Alliance facilitator took children off of school grounds to their home.[14] One of the boys attending was told that "his mother would not know if he attended a GSA conference and miss all of his classes," and at the conference he was given materials that included "a space ship shaped like a giant penis with a caption 'explore your anus'" and a comic-style flip-book

---

nized three unmarried adults as the legal parents of a child born within their 'polyamorous' family." Michael MacDonald, "3 Adults in Polyamorous Relationship Declared Legal Parents by N. L. Court," *CBC News*, June 14, 2018, https://www.cbc.ca/news/canada/newfoundland-labrador/polyamourous-relationship-three-parents-1.4706560.

12   Faust and Manning, *Them Before Us*, 80.

13   Faust and Manning, 79–80.

14   Lisa Corbella, "Corbella: Some Alarming Revelations About Two GSAs at Alberta Court of Appeal," *Calgary Herald*, December 4, 2018, https://calgaryherald.com/news/local-news/corbella-some-alarming-revelations-about-gsas-at-alberta-court-of-appeal. I have heard similar stories from BC.

that graphically illustrated gay sex between two males, one of whom looked far older than the other.[15]

It may be tempting to think of these examples as fringe occurrences or the result of misguided, but well-meaning counsellors. But this anti-parent approach, even if it will not be admitted, is intentional. One sex educator in the province of BC states that if a child has a different gender identity at school than they do at home, they do not tell the parents because they assume that if the parents have not been told, it is because the home must present a danger to that student.[16] One of the basic policy principles of BC's SOGI123 program is that children have the right of confidentiality, which clearly means the concealment of a child's sexual or gendered expression or experience from parents.[17] G. K. Chesterton's statement many years ago seems particularly pertinent in our day: "The State did not own men so entirely, even when it could send them to the stake, as it sometimes does now where it can send them to the elementary school."[18]

The case of a BC father, known to the courts as "CD," and his daughter is perhaps the preeminent example.[19] CD's daughter attended a public school which was among the first schools in the province to introduce SOGI123. In a difficult stage in early adolescence, she had been meeting with the school counsellor, which was at that time encouraged by her parents. Later on, however, CD discovered her gender identity change only when he saw a male name under her picture in

---

15   Corbella. The flipbook, which likely meets the legal definition of "child pornography," is called "Who's got the Condom," and is available from the BC Centre for Disease Control at http://www.bccdc.ca/resource-gallery/Documents/Educational%20 Materials/STI/Chee%20Mamuk/CPS_CheeMamuk_Order_Supply_BC.pdf.

16   Elisabeth Stitt, "The Parents' Round Table Talks LGBTQ - Kerri Isham Interview," *YouTube*, 2017, https://www.youtube.com/watch?v=tw2a9wVeNm0.

17   The ARC Foundation, "SOGI Policies & Procedures," *SOGI123*, https://bc.sogieducation.org/sogi1.

18   G. K. Chesterton, "St. Thomas More," in *The Collected Works of G. K. Chesterton. Vol. 3* (San Francisco: Ignatius Press, 1986). With thanks to Joe Boot, *Mission of God,* for this quote.

19   CD is the name used in court documents to anonymize the father. The following details are taken from a personal interview conducted Feb 12, 2022. See also Jeremiah Keenan, "Canadian Father Jailed For Talking About Court-Ordered Transgendering Of His Teenage Daughter," *The Federalist*, 2021, https://thefederalist.com/2021/03/26/canadian-father-jailed-for-talking-about-court-ordered-transgendering-of-his-teenage-daughter/.

her yearbook—a name, it was later revealed in court, that the school counsellor had helped her choose!

Things took a turn for the worse when the school counsellor recommended a local "expert" psychologist known for his gender-affirmative practices. Within two meetings, and in front of the thirteen-year-old minor, he stated that she was a "prime candidate for testosterone." CD's ex-wife was in favour, but CD was highly concerned at the rapidity of the diagnosis and recommended treatment, and was desperate for his daughter to see someone who did not seem like an activist. So when it was recommended that they consult at BC Children's Hospital, he was hopeful.

One day while at work CD received a concerned call from his ex-wife. She was there at Children's Hospital with their daughter—and they were about to give her the first injection of testosterone. Within no more than an hour after arriving, this irreversible treatment was going to begin. No significant mental evaluation. No second opinion. Just a single, short appointment.

Both parents agreed to forestall the process for at least a short while, but CD's wife was ultimately affirming of the treatment. In late 2018, the concerned father received a document that stated he had two weeks to challenge the treatment in court or she would begin the experimental treatment. Enclosed was a copy of the BC Infant's Act, which gives minors the legal right in the province to consent to medical procedures without parental permission.

Over the course of several court dates, and the escalation of the case to the BC Supreme Court, the father repeatedly ran afoul of the law. He refused, firstly, to adhere to a court-mandate that he use his daughter's preferred pronouns. A judge ruled this "family violence" and CD was threatened with arrest. This ruling was subsequently struck down at the BC Court of Appeals, but a gag order remained in place which prevented him from speaking to the media about the doctors and psychologists involved. Feeling that the stakes for his own daughter and other vulnerable children were simply too high, CD was imprisoned for six weeks for naming names. At every stage of this shocking ordeal, state institutions undermined the parental rights of this father trying to protect his daughter from making an irreversible and damaging medical decision at the tender age of fourteen.

Soon it may not just be the parents of gender-dysphoric children who have social workers or police knocking on their doors. The circumstances around the passing of Bill C-4, the so-called ban on "conversion therapy," is one of the most shocking events in recent Canadian political history. The bill's predecessor, C-6, was significantly challenged by the Conservative Party, and an enormous number of dissenting briefs were submitted from diverse viewpoints. However, a year later, with a more radical version of the same bill before them, not a *single* leader in either the House or the Senate voiced opposition to the bill, including all of the sixty-two Conservative MPs who had voted against the previous bill.[20]

The Sunday after the bill came into force, in January, 2022, thousands of pastors in both the United States and Canada preached sermons on biblical sexuality, including the condemnation of same-sex sexual behavior and transgender identity, in defiance of the bill, which could easily be understood to prohibit not only biblical counseling on these topics, but also scriptural preaching, and even parental counsel or house rules.[21] The precise legal implications are yet to be discovered, but if the wide impact of Canada's previous Bill C-16[22] is any measure, Christian pastors and parents in Canada may soon be fielding inquiries from the authorities for simply practicing and teaching the historic faith.

It is clear that sexual and gender identities now trump family identity. The state is not only increasingly pitting these two forces against each other, but it seems ready and willing to step in and enforce the subjugation of the family to the autonomous sexual self. No matter that the medical transition of the gender dysphoric is not effective long-

---

20   Flyn Ritchie, "Bill C-4 Criminalizes Conversion Therapy – Without Opposition," *BC Catholic*, 2021, https://bccatholic.ca/news/canada/bill-c-4-criminalizes-conversion-therapy-without-opposition.

21   Jon Brown, "Thousands of Churches Raise Alarm About Scope of New Canadian 'Conversion Therapy' Ban," *Fox News*, 2022, https://www.foxnews.com/world/thousands-churches-raise-alarm-scope-new-canadian-conversion-therapy-ban.

22   Bill C-16 added gender identity and gender expression to the Canadian Human Rights Act, and was passed on June 15, 2017 in the Senate.

term.[23] No matter that transgender identification is proving socially contagious in young women.[24] No matter that adverse mental and physical health outcomes for LGBT are strongly linked to childhood trauma.[25] No matter that non-heterosexuality is so fluid it is difficult to even conceive of sexuality as a stable identifier or category.[26] No matter that medical transition constitutes the most obscene and destructive sort of conversion therapy for same-sex attracted youth perhaps ever practiced.[27] Satan is hell-bent on destroying children and the family.

LOST MEN; LOST HOUSES

The family ought to be a hallowed haven in a hostile world. The warfare undermining this most fundamental of institutions takes place not only outside its walls, but increasingly inside as well. In the Old Testament, rest and pleasure was often communicated in metaphorical language of gardens, wells, or springs. The bonds of sexual union in marriage are also described using such language.

> Drink water from your own cistern, flowing water from your own well. Should your springs be scattered abroad, streams of water in the streets? Let them be for yourself alone, and not for strangers

---

23   Paul Dirks, "Transition as Treatment: The Best Studies Show the Worst Outcomes," *The Public Discourse*, 2020, https://www.thepublicdiscourse. com/2020/02/60143/. Among the studies cited in the above article, special note should be given to the important but horrifically misnamed, Ebba K Lindqvist et al., "Quality of Life Improves Early after Gender Reassignment Surgery in Transgender Women," *Europian Journal of Plastic Surgery* 40 (2017): 223–26, https://doi.org/10.1007/ s00238-016-1252-0.

24   Lisa Littman, "Parent Reports of Adolescents and Young Adults Perceived to Show Signs of a Rapid Onset of Gender Dysphoria," *PLoS One* 13, no. 8 (2018), https://doi.org/e0202330.

25   Paul Dirks, "The Empirical Case Against 'Conversion-Therapy' Bans," *The Public Discourse*, 2020, https://www.thepublicdiscourse.com/2020/03/60895/. Among the studies cited in the above article, see especially, Judith P Andersen and John Blosnich, "Disparities in Adverse Childhood Experiences among Sexual Minority and Heterosexual Adults," *PLoS One* 8, no. 1 (2013), https://doi.org/10.1371/journal. pone.0054691.

26   Paul Dirks, "Submission to the Standing Committee on Justice and Human Rights Respecting Bill C-6," 2020, https://www.ourcommons.ca/Content/Committee/432/JUST/Brief/BR10961898/br-external/DirksPaul-e.pdf. See also, Lisa M Diamond, "Sexual Fluidity in Male and Females," *Current Sexual Health Reports* 8 (2016): 249–56, https://doi.org/10.1007/s11930-016-0092-z.

27   Lisa Bildy, "Justice Centre Staff Lawyer Presenting to Parliamentary Standing Committee," *YouTube*, 2020, https://www.youtube.com/watch?v=2nic9J0wUpA.

with you. Let your fountain be blessed, and rejoice in the wife of your youth, a lovely deer, a graceful doe. Let her breasts fill you at all times with delight; be intoxicated always in her love. (Prv 5:15–19)

In Proverbs, Solomon warns his son over and over again to beware of forsaking the wife of his youth for the forbidden woman who roams the streets at night. The adulteress offers pleasure, but her bed is a place of death (Prv 2:18). The home is a place of sexual fidelity; the streets a place of sexual immorality.

These days the streets run right through our homes. The Internet carries with it an endless array of dark alleyways and evil paths, ensnaring and emasculating many of our men. Instead of investing their energies, interests, and bodies in a comprehensive, intimate union that builds up their families, they steal from their households in their disloyalty, betraying their wives and children. Pornography is a snare that has killed many a marriage, destroyed many a Christian witness, and made shipwreck of many a pastoral ministry. Pornography is an evil that is tantamount to adultery, and men ought to consider that unrepentant sin in this area is grounds for divorce. As Jesus teaches in Matthew 5:29, do *whatever it takes* to rid yourself of such evil, for the sexually immoral will not inherit the kingdom of God (Eph 5:5).

We live in a sex-obsessed culture. Music videos, clothing ads, Netflix, and ads on websites—even Christian websites—are often subtly or overtly immoral. The number of so-called Christians who watch the HBO fantasy series *Game of Thrones* (and its offshoots) is disturbing. The show is particularly known for gratuitous sexual imagery, including incest, orgies, and lesbian and gay sex scenes. It is simply unfathomable that a Christian man, concerned with pursuing the holiness of Christ, looking to invest his energies and interests in his wife and family, and seeking to put to death the deeds of the body (Rom 8:13), would put such abject filth willingly before his eyes. In contrast, righteous Job made a covenant with his eyes never to lust after a woman (Jb 31:1). The standard for our thought-life is clear in the word of God: "Whatever is true, whatever is honorable, whatever is just, whatever is pure, whatever is lovely, whatever is commendable, if there is any excellence, if there is anything worthy of praise, think about these things" (Phil 4:8).

Men—husbands and fathers—are one of the keys to the stability of the family and society. In our current culture it is somewhat provocative to simply state the scriptural truth that men are to be the heads of their homes (Eph 5:23). But the sociological data bears witness to the enormous harms within Western society when men do not take responsibility for their own homes, families, and children.

> We know the statistics – that children who grow up without a father are five times more likely to live in poverty and commit crime; nine times more likely to drop out of schools and 20 times more likely to end up in prison. They are more likely to have behavioral problems, or run away from home, or become teenage parents themselves. And the foundations of our community are weaker because of it. ... Of all the rocks upon which we build our lives... family is the most important. And we are called to recognize and honor how critical every father is to that foundation.[28]

These words were part of a Father's Day speech delivered in 2008 by then-Senator, Barack Obama. One wonders if he would give such a speech today, or if he would trip over himself to make the message more palatable to liberal egalitarianism. But the data was clear back then, and if anything, is even clearer now. As he summed up back in 2008, "We need fathers." When fathers are absent in society, everything goes wrong.

Rob Henderson knows this firsthand. Currently a doctoral candidate studying Social Psychology at Cambridge University, he had to navigate a difficult road to get there.[29] He never knew his father, and at three years of age he watched his mother being taken away in handcuffs. He was living out of garbage bags at age seven and smoking marijuana at nine. In his teen years, he started experimenting with drugs and was frequently absent from school, finishing with a 2.2 GPA. But then a male history teacher, an Air Force veteran, suggested he enlist in the Air Force. After serving, he attended Yale on the G.I.

---

28   Cited from Paul Kengor, *Takedown* (Washington, DC: WND Books, 2015), 14–15..

29   Rob Henderson, "America's Lost Boys and Me," *Common Sense*, November 2021, https://bariweiss.substack.com/p/americas-lost-boys-and-me?s=r.

Bill and has since accomplished significant work in the field of social psychology, including studying what he has coined "luxury beliefs": expensive, fashionable, status-granting beliefs that "can only be afforded by people whose status shields them from the harm those views can cause."[30] Drawing from both life experience and academic research, he concludes,

> There's one story that's neat and clean and politically convenient to tell about my life. It goes like this: Poverty is the root cause of my problems (and those of my friends). With enough financial aid, and a good test score, anything is possible. Including Yale. Or Cambridge. But the data tells quite a different story. Poverty, even extreme poverty, is surmountable. What is nearly impossible to overcome is the instability—the psychological havoc—created by broken homes. Especially for boys.[31]

The current crisis is a circular one for men—fathers are more likely to be absent from the home than mothers, and as Henderson notes in his article, boys suffer greater effects for this instability: "Single parenthood appears to be especially detrimental for boys, while having married parents is particularly advantageous."[32] A cycle of societal breakdown lies upon the backs of men, both as victims and perpetrators.

Society, however, has disincentivized family life for men. They are told that their masculinity is "toxic"—and not just when their authority is used for their own selfish purposes. Opening a door for a woman or the inherent instinct to cherish or protect a woman is presented as evidence of sexism.[33] There is no longer any unique call for men to provide for their families; no other-oriented reason to work hard and gain dominion.[34] On account of this, there is a crisis of non-working young men in Western society, a "Great Depression-scale

---

30   Henderson "America's Lost Boys and Me".

31   Henderson "America's Lost Boys and Me."

32   Henderson "America's Lost Boys and Me."

33   Peter Glick and Susan T. Fiske, "The Ambivalent Sexism Inventory: Differentiating Hostile and Benevolent Sexism," *Journal of Personality and Social Psychology* 70, no. 3 (1996): 491–512.

34   For an historically and scripturally balanced view on feminism, men, and the family, see Nancy Pearcey, *Total Truth* (Wheaton, IL: Crossway Books, 2005), 325–48.

underutilization of male manpower," as Nicholas Eberstadt makes clear in *Men Without Work*.[35] In prior generations, a man would be shamed for not working, but feminist ideology has largely removed this stigma[36] while government support and multiple family incomes make it a practical possibility.

On the flip side, there are few disincentives to keep men from checking out on their families. Got your girlfriend pregnant? Convince her to have an abortion. Marital life not going smoothly? Leave her with the children. Can't find a good job? Maybe your wife could go to work instead. When fathers are absent and demoted from their God-ordained role of headship, everyone loses. As Gad Saad quips in *The Parasitic Mind*, "It is perhaps not a good idea to pathologize half of humanity when dealing with a sexually reproducing species."[37]

IDENTITY AND THE FAMILY

The Bible is full of stories of men whose leadership—both good and bad—had long-standing repercussions on their families. One of my favorite Old Testament characters is Jonadab, the son of Rechab. We are introduced to Jonadab (or alternatively, Jehonadab) in a time of revolution, after the anointing of Jehu as king of Israel by Elisha. Jehu is chosen to be an instrument of the Lord's retribution, a role he fulfills with relish—his chariot functioning as a metonym for his zeal. In the midst of his violent reprisal against Ahab's family for their wickedness, Jehu meets Jonadab on the way to meting out justice.

> And he greeted him and said to him, "Is your heart true to my heart as mine is to yours?" And Jehonadab answered, "It is." Jehu said, "If it is, give me your hand." So he gave him his hand. And Jehu

---

35   Nicholas Eberstadt, *Men Without Work* (West Conshohocken, PA: Templeton Press, 2016), 18. "The spread and general social toleration of the workless lifestyle of men, of course, could not have taken place without a normative sea change as well. An earlier era had terms for sturdy men who chose to sit on the economic sidelines, living off the toil of others. None were kind or forgiving." Eberstadt, 38.

36   I am not stating, of course, that feminists explicitly argue that men should not work. Rather, I am arguing that the shame which would have provided the proverbial "kick in the pants" to men in prior generations has been removed as the family's financial provision is no longer seen as the unique responsibility of the man.

37   Saad, *The Parasitic Mind*, 87.

took him up with him into the chariot. And he said, "Come with me, and see my zeal for the LORD." So he had him ride in his chariot. (2 Kgs 10:15–16)

This same Jonadab is mentioned again in Jeremiah 35, where his descendants serve as a powerful object lesson in obedience. The Lord commanded the prophet Jeremiah to bring the Rechabites into the temple chambers and offer them wine. Their response?

> We will drink no wine, for Jonadab the son of Rechab, our father, commanded us, "You shall not drink wine, neither you nor your sons forever. You shall not build a house; you shall not sow seed; you shall not plant or have a vineyard; but you shall live in tents all your days, that you may live many days in the land where you sojourn." We have obeyed the voice of Jonadab the son of Rechab, our father, in all that he commanded us, to drink no wine all our days, ourselves, our wives, our sons, or our daughters. (Jer 35:6–8)

Putting these passages together, it seems that Jonadab was a man known for his great piety, which for him and his family involved degrees of separation from the world. Jehu, the new king, wanted to enlist this righteous figure to his cause, and so he offered his hand, which Jonadab took. We do not know how long these two walked in concert. Jehu probably did not live up to Jonadab's expectations even within their lifetimes— "Jehu was not careful to walk in the law of the LORD" (2 Kgs 10:31)—but it was the generations of these two men which stands out in particular contrast. Whereas Jehu's descendants were unfaithful to God, Jonadab's descendants were still obeying him and the Lord two hundred and fifty years later in the time of Jeremiah. Not only were they keeping faith with God, but remarkably they were still obeying the extra laws to which Jonadab had enjoined them.

We are in desperate need of this kind of multi-generational gospel success. Like the Rechabites, we need a family identity strong enough that our children, and our children's children, are not swayed by the compromise of those around them, even of other Christians. In the West, we are particularly weak when it comes to forging familial identity and so our children become easy pickings for the Beastly world system. I remember a conversation about family several years ago with a Hindu friend in our neighbourhood. We were walking as we spoke, but at one point he stopped, turned to me, and said, "respectfully, Canadians do not know anything about family." Strong words. But as a generalization, he was correct.

As I have noted, some blame for the present predicament of the home may rest upon a culture which tries to tear down familial identity through the multiplication and promotion of other identities, including sexual ones. Much of the blame, however, rests with families and churches. We have failed to be intentional in building a family identity. Ironically, you cannot take the least step into the world of business or leadership without hearing talk of mission, vision, values, goals, and strategic plans. But only rarely does one hear of similar ideals applied to the family.

Those who do not have a cultural or ethnic identity as part of their family identity may be particularly vulnerable to fragmentation, as illustrated by a fascinating opinion piece published by *The Globe & Mail* in 2017.[38] In it, a Vancouver mother narrates the discovery of her Kindergarten daughter's anxieties about her whiteness. "I wish I wasn't white....All we've ever done is hurt people...I wish my skin was dark and that I had a culture."[39] The mother's solution was to introduce her daughter to her English cultural heritage by teaching her the tradition of high tea.

> I explain that high tea must be served right at 4 o'clock, not a minute sooner, and that sandwiches are to be cut twice on the diagonal with crusts removed in their entirety. "Why?" she asks to all of the above. "It's just our culture." Later in the week, Abigail replicates the high-tea ritual for her teddies and dolls, and then in a crowning act of glory for her Mexican playmate next door. "It's from my culture".[40]

A girl who had no national or ethnic identity, swimming in a culture that undermines familial identity, was left despondent about who she was—at five years of age! Although the full article suggests to

---

38   Tama Ward, "Postcolonial Parenting," *Globe and Mail*, October 4, 2017, https://www.theglobeandmail.com/life/facts-and-arguments/how-can-i-raise-an-enlightened-child-without-depriving-my-daughter-of-her-culturalroots/article36484338/.

39   Ward "Postcolonial Parenting".

40   Ward "Postcolonial Parenting".

me that the mother was part of the initial problem, her solution evidences considerable insight.

There is a secret power built into family life that is subtle enough that many people miss it, but strong enough to help the family withstand the onslaught of the world—ritual, and its close cousin, routine. Routines are the structure of family life, the bones upon which the musculature of individual and corporate action are built. Routines are part of the stewardship of family "time, space, and resources."[41] They are ordinary and repetitive, and yet it is precisely these factors which provide their power. Meals are among the most obvious routines. Most people will eat three times a day, at around the same times. This structure helps us make the most use of the day, divided as it is into three or four sections. For instance, there are the things we routinely do before breakfast. We are told to meditate upon Scripture and pray early in the morning (Ps 5:3, 88:13, 147–148). We may also exercise our bodies first thing, or read. After breakfast we get to the main work of the day, and usually continue at it after a break at lunch. After supper there may be time for other pursuits, whether related to personal projects, church life, or hobbies. The routine of three meals a day keeps our life ordered and fresh for new tasks and obligations. Weekly routines are helpful too. Children are greatly benefitted by order, even if it is the simple knowledge of what happens on which days of the week, to be able to state, for instance, that "Sunday is for church and God."

Rituals are also, in the largest sense, routines, but they are more significant and symbolic in that they have a religious quality and provide a narrative for the "we" of family. Rituals may include family traditions around special days or festivals which occur weekly or yearly, or those which concern significant life events—weddings, births, baptisms, etc. They can be as small as praying and blessing your children every night before bed, or as large as a rite-of-passage ceremony. Those who are religious tend towards ritual—they have a clearer sense than atheists or agnostics of what the story and meaning of life is which binds together the otherwise disparate parts of existence and

---

41   Sharon Denham, "Relationship Between Family Rituals, Family Routines, and Health," *Journal of Family Nursing* 9, no. 3 (2003): 305–30.

action. The Old Testament law enjoined just such a set of symbolic structures in the feasts and festivals which were to be carried out in family units (Dt 14:26).

Parents ought to look for opportunities within the structure of days, weeks, years, holidays, and special events, to intentionally build a family identity. Choose at least one time a day for family worship where the household reads and memorizes Scripture, sings hymns, and prays together. Make bedtime notable in some significant and spiritual way. Read a bit of Christian literature at the supper table. Protect the Sabbath from the mundane. Have a special restaurant you visit at Easter, Thanksgiving, or Christmas. Or a particular place you visit every summer. Almost any routine or ritual is better than none in building family identity.

Furthermore, think strategically about your family values, goals, and identity. What makes your family different than others? Not *better*, but unique. And what does God want your family to accomplish together for His glory? A friend of mine suggests that a family may want to put together a family shield that pictorially communicates the values of the family, something our family has recently done. In *The Promise of Jonadab*, E. Ray and Gail Pinckney Moore suggest having a family covenant and home rules.[42] Their own home rules are:

1. Family celebrations, traditions
2. Brothers and sisters regarded as permanent friends
3. Regular worship, Bible study, quiet time and Scripture memory
4. Supper together around the table without a television
5. Short accounts when we have sinned
6. Practical holiness
7. Correction for disobedience, disrespect, stealing and lying
8. Home schooling or Christian schooling
9. Showing respect for parents and others in authority.[43]

Building an identity in Christ is the ultimate goal, but it is an

---

42   E. Ray Moore and Gail Pinckney Moore, *The Promise of Jonadab* (Greenville, SC: Ambassador International, 2010), chaps. 105–120.

43   Moore and Moore, *The Promise of Jonadab,* 119.

instructive and protective steppingstone for a child to have a family identity as well. The structure of Israel in the Old Testament exhibits this truth. Each member of Israel was part of an adopted nation—out of Egypt God called His son (Ex 4:22–23, Hos 11:1). At the same time, there was a strong tribal identity. Each tribe had its inheritance and its chiefs. When it came time for war, the nation would go out by their tribes and families. Family identity was not a hindrance in time of battle, but a help.

The Resistance Cell

The church I pastor is not very large, but it is diverse (not to mention faithful and courageous), and I learn tremendously from the counsel and viewpoints of my Lao, Filipino, and Brazilian brothers and sisters. East Europeans and Russians are also well-represented in our church. These saints tend to hold fast to the truth, speak plainly, and never back down from their convictions. Their perspective and experience coming from Communist backgrounds has been especially helpful over the last few years as they have warned their brothers and sisters of the creeping totalitarianism which they see in North America. When they say, "you do not realize what is coming," I pay attention.

It is this cultural background and wisdom from which Rod Dreher draws in *Live Not By Lies* in order to prepare Christians and conservatives for what may be coming soon to our own shores, even if the totalitarianism gaining a foothold here may not look identical to its Communist counterpart. In the book, Dreher describes the family as a "resistance cell," a purposeful anti-totalitarian unit able not only to protect the faith of the children, but to train them to be change-agents as well.[44] One of the families Dreher offers as an example is that of Václav and Kamila Benda, faithful Catholics who lived in Prague, Czechoslovakia during Communist rule. They were outcasts in their own country because of their faith, but their children viewed the difference between themselves and other children as "a value and not

---

44   Rod Dreher, *Live Not By Lies : A Manual for Christian Dissdents* (New York: Sentinel, 2020), 129–50.

something bad."[45] Dreher writes,

> They brought them up to understand that they, as Christians, were not going to go along to get along in their totalitarian society. Vaclav and Kamila knew that if they did not strongly impart that sense of difference to their children, they risked losing them to propaganda and to widespread conformity to the totalitarian system.[46]

Patrik, one of their six children, describes how their parents were heroes in their eyes, demanding obedience and family solidarity against the evils outside their doors. "Sometimes it was hard," he relates, "but it made us stronger."[47] Strength of conviction and character are forged in the fires of difficulty, and the life of the home provides security for the struggle we face outside of it.

This remarkable resistance cell not only functioned as the fortress and training ground for those within it, however. Many others found strength and hospitality there. The Benda's did not shutter their windows and withdraw from society, as many others did.[48] Václav insisted that "the family does not exist for its own purpose but for the service of something beyond itself."[49] Instead, their home became a place of briefing after the enemy had interrogated other resistance fighters, and an anti-propaganda academy where movies and books with "dangerous" content were encountered and openly discussed. It was a righteous outpost in the enemy's territory. Home ought to be a haven; it also ought to be a headquarters.

The Marxists and the Maker

The Beast's worldwide power described in the book of Revelation is a particularly diabolical form of totalitarianism. In order to bring about this anti-Christ global dominion, the devil must destroy the traditional

---

45   Dreher, *Live Not By Lies,* 139.

46   Dreher, *Live Not By Lies,* 139.

47   Dreher, *Live Not By Lies,* 139.

48   Dreher, *Live Not By Lies,* 150.

49   Dreher, *Live Not By Lies,* 149. See the section, "Escape to the Hills?" in chapter 6 as well.

family. It will be the traditional totalitarian playbook on steroids. That playbook is mostly written already: redefine marriage into nothing, corrupt it through immorality, pit children against parents, chop off its head and leadership, and undermine its solidarity.

Totalitarian states have always attacked the family. Paul Kengor, an historian of Communism, chronicles how blatant this attack has been in the past. Early American socialist Robert Owen (1771–1858) considered marriage as one of an unholy trinity, together with private property and religion, of "monstrous evils."[50] Karl Marx famously included the "abolition of the family" as a central tenet of Communism in his *Communist Manifesto*. Friedrich Engels was even more radical, teaching that one of the benefits of the liberation of women from the economic bondage of home life was unconstrained sexual license.

Lenin and Stalin wholeheartedly adopted the anti-family sexual-license ideas of Marx and Engels. An article published by an anonymous Russian woman in *The Atlantic* in 1926 states that the Bolsheviks "regarded the family, like every other 'bourgeois' institution, with fierce hatred, and set out with a will to destroy it."[51] She describes how the relaxation of divorce and abortion laws led to the extreme proliferation of both. Divorce was rampant, ballooning to "levels unseen in human history."[52] Kengor notes that one study from the 1960s reported that it was not unusual to meet Soviets "who had been married and divorced upwards of fifteen times."[53] The effect this attack on the family had upon children was particularly horrific. "By 1934 Moscow women were having three abortions for every live birth," a statistic as staggering as it is sobering.[54] The family-destroying totalitarians were not just public theorists either, they were private practitioners as well. Almost to a person, they left behind them a wake of relational ruin as

---

50   Kengor, *Takedown*, 25.

51   "A Woman Resident in Russia", "The Russian Effort to Abolish Marriage," *The Atlantic*, July 1926, https://www.theatlantic.com/magazine/archive/1926/07/the-russian-effort-to-abolish-marriage/306295/.

52   Kengor, *Takedown*, 44.

53   Kengor, *Takedown*, 45.

54   Kengor, *Takedown*, 45.

they engaged in abuse, adultery, and open relationships.[55]

But there is hope. God too has a playbook. In it there are both promises and prophecies concerning our families. Firstly, God has promised us our children. Traditions like the Baptist one in which I grew up do not tend to hold as tightly to these promises as they ought. But they are given to us as a sure foundation for family life—a foundation in God and in His covenant with us.

> "And as for me, this is my covenant with them," says the LORD: "My Spirit that is upon you, and my words that I have put in your mouth, shall not depart out of your mouth, or out of the mouth of your offspring, or out of the mouth of your children's offspring," says the LORD, "from this time forth and forevermore." (Is 59:21)

We ought to pray these promises back to God, holding fast in faith that God will do what He has promised while we give ourselves to our responsibilities in training up our children in the way they should go, so that when they mature, they do not depart from that path (Prv 22:6). As Peter preached at Pentecost, the promise of the gospel is for us *and* for our children (Acts 2:39).

We have great promises, but as we look to an end that is sure to come one day, there is also glorious prophecy. I believe that a right interpretation of Revelation and other last-days passages reveals that a time of future revival will concur with a time of great tribulation as the world takes sides in the final conflict. Romans 11 too suggests at least one more great worldwide revival, as a great ingathering of the Jews—to the degree that Paul states "all Israel will be saved"—takes place through jealousy, as Israel see God's great power in a saving work among the Gentiles.[56] It can be safely inferred, therefore, that the prior Gentile work must be as commensurately great as the subsequent Jewish revival it provokes.

---

55   For the tawdry historical details, see especially chapters 5 and 14 in Kengor, *Takedown.*

56   Jealousy is a clear element in Rom 11:11 and 14 as Paul speaks of present ministry, however, it is also inferred in Rom 11:30 ("in order that by the mercy shown to you they also may [now] receive mercy") after the topic of the future ingathering of the Jews is broached. My interpretation is somewhat, but not completely, dependent on whether or not the variant "now" (νῦν) is included in verse 30. For a discussion, see the NET Bible translation notes on Rom 11:30. Biblical Studies Press, *The NET Bible*, First Edition (Biblical Studies Press, 2005).

What does this future revival have to do with the family? Much. Revival is not a completely unique work, but rather, as Jonathan Edwards wrote, "a remarkable outpouring of the Spirit in a special season of mercy."[57] It intensifies the normative work of the Holy Spirit in the regular means of grace such as preaching and prayer. It is not surprising, then, that revivals are marked by the same sorts of things which attend Christian maturity and growth, but carried out to a greater extent or brought about rapidly. The life of the family is not only an intrinsic part of Christian growth, but as we noted at the outset of the chapter, the first and most fundamental part of the expansion of the Lord's kingdom. In times of revival, this family blessing and growth is heightened.

Consider the revival brought about by John the Baptist which heralded the coming of the kingdom. It is described in the gospels this way: "And he will turn many of the children of Israel to the Lord their God, and he will go before him in the spirit and power of Elijah, to turn the hearts of the fathers to the children, and the disobedient to the wisdom of the just, to make ready for the Lord a people prepared" (Lk 1:16–17). At Pentecost, Peter preached from the prophet Joel that in the last days God would pour out his Spirit on all flesh, "and your sons and your daughters shall prophesy." In keeping with the truth of these passages, many revivals in church history have begun with, or incorporated, children.

In *Children and Revival*, Harry Sprange provides ample historical evidence of God using children in the revivals of Scotland. As one example, there was a period of religious awakening in Scotland from 1859 to 1863 following the New York prayer meetings started by Jeremy Lamphier. In these years, revivals were sparked in certain towns by the public prayers of teenagers,[58] countless prayer meetings were started and maintained for children by other children,[59] entire classrooms

---

57   Jonathan Edwards, *The Works of President Edwards* (Worcester: Isaiah Thomas, June 1808), 38.

58   Harry Sprange, *Children in Revival: 300 Years of God's Work in Scotland* (Geanies House: Christian Focus Publications, 2002), 159.

59   Sprange, *Children in Revival*, 138.

and Sabbath schools turned to the Lord under forceful conviction,[60] and children led their parents to the Lord.[61] There are accounts of young boys leading family worship where the father was unwilling,[62] and of girls enduring beatings at home in order to attend prayer meetings or revival services.[63]

We ought not be surprised. God has promised us our children. This is why the family is under attack. A child was to be the redeemer of the world and the destroyer of the devil's fruit (Gn 3:15). It is "out of the mouth of babies and infants" that God has established strength to "still the enemy and the avenger" (Ps 8:2). And one day the serpent will be put under the dominion of the smallest child— "the child shall play over the hole of the cobra" (Is 11:7). The dragon will never fully devour the family, but you must do your part by God's grace and power. Put in your "home-work."

---

60 Sprange, *Children in Revival*, 139–40.

61 Sprange, *Children in Revival*, 171.

62 Sprange, *Children in Revival*, 130.

63 Sprange, *Children in Revival*, 131.

Apocalypse-Preparation List

- Embrace the blessings and challenges of expanding God's dominion through children and the family.
- Guard your marital life through sexual fidelity. Fully repent of viewing pornography or entertaining unholy thoughts.
- Husbands: embrace your role in providing for, protecting, and promoting your family—you are crucial.
- Intentionally use family routine and ritual to communicate family identity.
- Develop a family shield, mission statement, and/or house rules.
- Do not be afraid to make "us" and "them" distinctions with your family—it can be protective. Think strategically about your family as a resistance cell.
- Pray God's promises concerning the long-term kingdom-success of your family.
- Memorize Psalm 127. "Unless the LORD builds the house, those who build it labor in vain. Unless the LORD watches over the city, the watchman stays awake in vain. It is in vain that you rise up early and go late to rest, eating the bread of anxious toil; for he gives to his beloved sleep. Behold, children are a heritage from the LORD, the fruit of the womb a reward. Like arrows in the hand of a warrior are the children of one's youth. Blessed is the man who fills his quiver with them! He shall not be put to shame when he speaks with his enemies in the gate."

CHAPTER 5

Practice Pioneering

THE KINGS WHO BUILT

Darius the Great of Persia needed a new capital. He had, together
with six other conspirators, taken the throne of Persia from a usurper,
Guamata, who had stepped into its vacancy upon the death of Cyrus'
son Cambyses. Darius did not have a hereditary right to the throne, but
his was an ancient family, and he had been the king's spear-bearer.[1] In
the aftermath of Cambyses' death, he spent several years putting down
insurrections and revolts within his new dominion. Although successful in warfare, the new king excelled in administration. In his reorga-
nization of the empire he first established Susa as his administrative
centre, rebuilding it and its citadel, before finally turning to build a new
capital—a new city altogether.[2] He called it and the region surrounding
it Parsa, but it was to be known in history as Persepolis.[3]

     Built upon a rock outcropping, it loomed fifty to sixty feet
above the plain below.[4] The city's curtain wall, connecting its towers,
were thirty-three feet thick and on the inside of these walls was the gar-
rison of the famed Immortals.[5] Although impressively secure, the new
capital was built by the king to be a place of beauty and wonder. One
historian effused that "there has been nothing in all Asia as sumptuous

---

1   A. T. Olmstead, *History of the Persian Empire* (Chicago: University of
Chicago Press, 1978), 107.

2   Olmstead, *History of the Persian Empire*, 166.

3   Olmstead, *History of the Persian Empire*, 173.

4   Olmstead, *History of the Persian Empire*, 173–74.

5   Olmstead, *History of the Persian Empire*, 174.

as Persepolis."[6] The enormous Apadana, the audience hall of Darius, had seventy-two columns which soared in height to almost 80 feet and had ornately carved bull-capitals. The Tacara, Darius' palace, like so many other places in his city, contained reliefs and friezes that were brilliant in color,[7] and was in some places so highly polished that it has been called the "Hall of Mirrors."[8] The ancient historian Didorus described Persepolis as "the richest city under the sun," and that "the private houses had been furnished with every sort of wealth over the years."[9] Such was the legendary affluence of Persepolis that when Alexander took the city in 330 BC, its treasuries were so full of silver and gold that he had to import thousands of baggage animals from Babylon to carry them off.[10]

From a biblical perspective, what is fascinating is that much of Darius' blessing may have come on account of his relationship to the Jews and it is likely, according to James B. Jordan and others, that he is both the Persian monarch depicted in the book of Esther and at the beginning of Nehemiah— "the queen sitting beside him" (Neh 2:6).[11]

As in the accounts of Darius the Great, the recorded histories of the kings of Judah and Israel also depict an emphasis upon building as one of several evidences of successful and godly dominion under God. [12] In 2 Chronicles 26, for example, we are told that King Uzziah built cities (v6), built and fortified towers (v9), cut out cisterns (v10), organized the army and built for them armaments (v11–14) and

---

6   A. W. Lawrence, "The Acropolis and Persepolis," *The Journal of Hellenistic Studies* 71 (1951): 111, https://www.jstor.org/stable/628191.111.

7   A. Shapur Shahbazi, "Persepolis," in *Encyclopedia Iranica*, 2012, http://www.iranicaonline.org/articles/persepolis.

8   Olmstead, *History of the Persian Empire*, 184.

9   Cited from Shahbazi, "Persepolis."

10   G. Stott, "Persepolis," *Greece & Rome* 7, no. 20 (1938): 71–72, https://www.jstor.org/stable/641657.

11   James B. Jordan, "The Chronology of Ezra & Nehemiah, Part 1," *Theopolis Institute*, February 1991, https://theopolisinstitute.com/the-chronology-of-ezra-nehemiah-part-1/.

12   Most of the accounts have a summary statement of God's moral judgment of the king, followed by three themes in the narrative: the king's relationship to worship, the king's relationship to the kingdom itself, often in building, and the king's relationship to warfare and other nations. This may be triadic or tri-perspectival, evidencing upward, inward, and outward orientations of their dominion under God.

through "skillful men" made machines of war (v14). These are presented as evidence of God's blessing as he sought the Lord (v5). In contrast, the Chaos-forces of the world are constantly tearing down what
is good. Although there are times in which this destruction is accomplished by brute force, like the siege engines of a great empire bom-
barding a solitary city, more often it is by slow erosion, like thieves
picking away at walls left in disrepair.

We have remarked several times already that man's dominion
under God is to be comprehensive. It is also to be progressive—not in
the sense of the modern anti-God ideology, but in the sense of a continual project. In the original good creation, the raw materials of the earth
were to be harnessed to build and extend man's reach for the glory of
God over earth. But sin presented new obstacles and dilemmas to these
works: evil edifices opposed to God's kingdom, and destructive forces
deployed to tear down the good works.

The call of Abraham (Gn 12:1–3) is a pivotal passage in
Scripture which finds its fruition not only in the nation of Israel, but
also in the people of the New Covenant. It is possible to miss an
important connection if we begin the story of Abraham at Genesis
12, however. The archetypal man of faith had to leave somewhere in
order to have (and become) a new beginning. Narratively, the place
he left was Babel.[13] The city and tower of Babel was a monument to
the achievements of a powerful world-builder by the name of Nimrod
(Gn 10:8–12). In contravention to the command of God to spread out
over the world, people gathered under him on the plains of Shinar to
build for themselves a tall tower that would extend to the heavens and
display their glory and ingenuity (Gn 11:4). And in a perverted sense, it
worked—until God intervened. He multiplied their languages, con-
fused their tongues, and sent them scampering off to the four corners of
the world.

This is the context in which we are to read the call of Abraham.
He must leave the place of human power, industry, and government, to

---

13   "The ruins of the tower and city of Babel loom in the background throughout the stories of Abraham, Isaac, and Jacob." Peter J. Leithart, *A House for My Name:
A Survey of the Old Testament* (Moscow, ID: Canon Press, 2000), 60.

build something new—a new people in a new city. In one sense it was a heavenly city to which he was looking, a place built by God (Heb 11:16). But as in our day, a heavenward orientation has very practical implications for what we build upon the earth.[14]

We have considered in the last few chapters how to build our own lives and our families. Here we want to turn to the outward work of building, to the pioneering of businesses, institutions, movements, networks, and even cities.

DILAPIDATED BUILDINGS

There are several reasons the Christian ought to be committed to the practice of pioneering. Fundamentally, there is always a need for new structures when the kingdom of God is growing. Church planting, even in a city with many churches, is usually good—we need more ministry. We need more evangelism, more discipleship, more teaching, and more worship. In addition to this fundamental need for new projects, many institutions seem to have a limited lifespan. This truth is sometimes hard to accept. When good people put their energy, time, and resources into an endeavour, it is painful to see it die. But the end of a project is not always negative. The need or reason for that structure or organization may simply have ceased. The expiration, however, often creates the need for something new. For these and other reasons, a pioneering mindset should be a constant for God's people.

However, there are reasons to believe that pioneering is particularly crucial at this present time. Preparations must be made for the dark days ahead, and to secure a strong future for the kingdom.

The prophetic literature provides a vocabulary that we need for this particular time when many structures in society, even Christian ones, lie in ruins. The exile of Israel to Babylon, and her subsequent return, is the occasion for much of the language we find in the Prophets about ruin and renovation. In the prophet Isaiah, for instance, we read

---

14   Furthermore, the vision of the new heavens and earth keep us from dichotomous thinking upon the subject. What we build here for Christ's glory will last eternally, in one form or another.

already in chapter 1 verse 7, "Your country lies desolate; your cities are burned with fire." In Isaiah 5:9, God categorically declares, "Surely many houses shall be desolate, large and beautiful houses, without inhabitant." Isaiah's prophetic calling, in fact, included a proclamation-induced hardening that was to continue "until cities lie waste without inhabitant, and houses without people, and the land is a desolate waste" (Is 6:10–11).

The joyful return of Israel from exile is portrayed using a similar structural metaphor: "Enlarge the place of your tent, and let the curtains of your habitations be stretched out; do not hold back; lengthen your cords and strengthen your stakes. For you will spread abroad to the right and to the left, and your offspring will possess the nations and will people the desolate cities" (Is 54:2–3).

Like an untended house, many Christian organizations and ministries lie in a state of dilapidation. Christian schools are a pertinent example, as many of them are currently following in the footsteps of higher education institutions such as Harvard and Yale which long ago left their historic Protestant roots.

Harvard, the first school of its kind in North America, was founded by Puritans in 1636 to train ministers.[15] Princeton University was conceived in revival, having its beginnings in the First Great Awakening of the eighteenth-century.[16] Yale held fast to the historic faith as Harvard drifted towards Unitarianism in the early nineteenth century, sending out its graduates throughout America, many of whom would hold influential positions in other seats of higher education, earning Yale the reputation as "mother of colleges." [17] Yet, all of these institutions are now thoroughly secularized.

Francis Schaeffer's warning in *The Great Evangelical Disas-*

---

15   W. C. Ringenberg, "Harvard University," in *Dictionary of Christianity in America* (InterVarsity Press, 1990).

16   W. C. Ringenberg, "Princeton University," in *Dictionary of Christianity in America* (InterVarsity Press, 1990).

17   W. C. Ringenberg, "Yale University and Divinity School," in *Dictionary of Christianity in America* (InterVarsity Press, 1990).

ter, his last book, written nearly forty years ago now, is worth citing at length:

> In every academic discipline the temptation and pressure to accommodate is overwhelming. Evangelicals were right in their rejection of a poor pietism which shut Christianity up into a very narrow area of spiritual life. Evangelicals were right in emphasizing the Lordship of Christ over all areas of culture—art, philosophy, society, government, academics, and so on. But then what happened? Many young evangelicals heard this message, went out into the academic world, and earned their undergraduate and graduate degrees from the finest secular schools. But something happened in the process. In the midst of totally humanistic colleges and universities, and a totally humanistic orientation in the academic disciplines, many of these young evangelicals began to be infiltrated by the anti-Christian world view which dominated the thinking of their colleges and professors. In the process, any distinctively evangelical Christian point of view was accommodated to the secularistic thinking in their discipline and to the surrounding world spirit of our age. To make the cycle complete, many of these have now returned to teach at evangelical colleges where what they present in their classes has very little that is distinctively Christian.[18]

Trinity Western University (TWU), in Langley, BC, is one such institution. The largest liberal arts university in Canada, they were recently champions of Christian conviction, boldly defending its scripturally based community covenant in the Canadian court system in its desire to launch a law school.[19] But for some time the institution has been rotting from the inside out.

Late in 2019, parental-rights activist Kari Simpson unearthed the video of an educators panel hosted by the UBC Faculty of Education called "Faith and Family: Navigating SOGI Inclusion in Schools." In it, Dr. Allyson Jule, the Dean of Education at TWU at the time, affirmed her support for BC's SOGI123 program, gay-straight alliances, and same-sex marriage. In the spring of 2020, I and several local pas-

---

18   Schaeffer, *The Complete Works*, 385.

19   Kathleen Harris, "Trinity Western Loses Fight for Christian Law School as Court Rules Limits on Religious Freedom 'Reasonable,'" *CBC News*, June 15, 2018, https://www.cbc.ca/news/politics/trinity-western-supreme-court-decision-1.4707240; "Supreme Court Rules Against TWU, Placing Public Perception Over Rule of Law," *ARPA Canada*, June 15, 2018, https://arpacanada.ca/articles/supreme-court-rules-against-twu-placing-public-perception-over-rule-of-law/.

tors expressed our concern to TWU that a department head tasked with teaching the future generation of Christian teachers was anti-scriptural in her approach to sexuality, gender, and marriage. Thankfully, these and other concerns seem to have been heeded. The *Mars' Hill Newspaper*, which is sympathetic to Jule and her views, reported her resignation from TWU in March of 2022.[20]

Sadly, there have been other indications that this was not an isolated situation. On March 10, 2022, an email went out to a TWU mailing list promoting an event titled "#BreakTheBias: Empowering women to succeed and allies to support." The brief notice contained the kind of intersectional and woke jargon typical of secular organizations— "allyship," "diverse line up of speakers," and "inclusive environments." But more provocative was the statement, "if you identify as a woman," and the notice that the presenters represented "BIPOC and LGBTQ+ perspectives."

As one TWU professor, who prefers to remain anonymous, remarked in a personal interview, there is currently a battle for the Christian soul of the institution as certain faculty members and staff are sacrificing the core of the gospel on the altar of political correctness. Many professors deny the historicity of Adam and Eve, the reality of original sin, and biblical teaching on sexual morality.[21] This educator illustrated TWU as a rowboat out at sea, unmoored, and far away from safe harbor. Although there are several excellent and trustworthy teachers at TWU, parents, students, and donors need to be forewarned that it is not a comprehensively "Christian" institution at present. Will it turn around and once again seek the haven of the historic faith and practice? May God grant His blessing to those working hard to steer the ship back to shore.

We are in desperate need of new, robustly Christian educational institutions. At pivotal moments in the past, church leaders understood the importance of building God-honoring, Scripture-teaching,

20 Carter Sawatsky, "Was It Something I Said? : How One of TWU's Most Decorated Deans Went from Star to Sunset," *Mars' Hill Newspaper*, March 23, 2022, https://www.marshillnewspaper.com/20220104_articles/was-it-something-i-said.

21 According to this professor, not only are there fellow faculty members who equivocate on gay marriage, but even on premarital sex.

discipline-inculcating schools. In the time of the Protestant Reformation, Martin Luther, faced with a German educational system that
was in shambles, advocated for the renewal of a thoroughly Christian
education.[22] He counseled families to keep their children in school,
instructed leaders to educate girls along with boys, and incited councilmen to build, sponsor, and reform schools and universities.[23]

For Luther, the priority in education was always the Word of
God.

> I am much afraid that the universities will prove to be the
> great gates of hell, unless they diligently labour in explaining the Holy
> Scriptures, and engraving them in the hearts of youth. I advise no one
> to place his child where the Scriptures do not reign paramount. Every
> institution in which men are not unceasingly occupied with the Word
> of God must become corrupt.[24]

Although Luther was pre-eminently concerned with the souls
of men and the state of the church, he also argued from the perspective
of the success of the state. He reasoned that for the sake of the broader
society there needed to be not only a return to Scripture, but also to the
diligence exhibited in the classical educational approach of the Greeks
and Romans. "Their system produced intelligent, wise, and competent
men," he counselled, "so skilled in every art and rich in experience that
if all the bishops, priests, and monks in the whole of Germany today
were rolled into one, you would not have the equal of a single Roman
soldier.[25] Theorizing that if it were somehow the case that there were
no eternal souls as stake, still, he wrote,

> this one consideration alone would be sufficient to justify the
> establishment everywhere of the very best schools for both boys and
> girls, namely, that in order to maintain its temporal estate outwardly

---

22   Martin Luther, "To the Councilmen of All Cities in Germany That They
Establish and Maintain Christian Schools," in *Luther's Works, Vol. 45*, ed. Jaroslav Jan
Pelikan (Philadelphia: Fortress Press, 1999), 342.

23   John E. Hill, "Luther on Education," *Consortium for Classical Lutheran
Education*, 2007, http://www.ccle.org/luther-on-education/.

24   Merle D'Aubigne, *History of the Reformation in the Sixteenth Century*,
trans. Henry Beveridge (Glasgow: William Collins, 1862), 71, https://archive.org/
details/historyofreform02merluoft.

25   Luther, "To the Councilmen," 356.

the world must have good and capable men and women, men able to rule well over land and people, women able to manage the household and train children and servants aright. Now such men must come from our boys, and such women from our girls. Therefore, it is a matter of properly educating and training our boys and girls to that end.[26]

Luther's reforms and advocacy largely worked, leading to a revival in Christian education which reverberated down throughout the centuries. We are in need of similar reform in these dark days. We must build while we can.

AN ALTERNATIVE CULTURE

It may be much more difficult to build in the days to come due to the very real possibility of societal ostracization. We are warned in Revelation 13:16–17 that the false prophet "causes all, both small and great, both rich and poor, both free and slave, to be marked on the right hand or the forehead, so that no one can buy or sell unless he has the mark, that is, the name of the beast or the number of its name." This pattern of the social ostracization of Christians has occurred multiple times in human history and the likelihood of another, more serious occurrence, is rapidly approaching.

For several years, major world organizations like the United Nations and the World Economic Forum, central banks, and many sovereign nations have been working to push and deploy a global biometric digital identity in order to achieve Goal 16.9 of the UN Sustainable Goals by 2030.[27] This digital identity will be linked to virtually every aspect of life: healthcare, mobility, food, financial services, government services, telecommunications, and social platforms.[28] This proof

---

26   Luther, "To the Councilmen," 368.

27   Canadian Banker's Association, "White Paper: Canada's Digital ID Future - A Federated Approach," 2018, https://cba.ca/embracing-digital-id-in-canada; Julie Dawson and Cristian Duda, "How Digital Identity Can Improve Lives in a Post-COVID-19 World," World Economic Forum, 2021, https://www.weforum.org/agenda/2021/01/davos-agenda-digital-identity-frameworks/.

28   Anne Josephine Flanagan and Sheila Warren, "Advancing Digital Agency: The Power of Data Intermediaries," World Economic Forum, February 15, 2022, https://www.weforum.org/reports/advancing-digital-agency-the-power-of-data-intermediaries.

of identity will not just be a card we carry in our pockets. Technology and web applications will increasingly blur the lines between our data, our time, our bodies, and our minds. "What the Fourth Industrial Revolution will lead to," Klaus Schwab stated at the Chicago Council of Global Affairs in 2019, "is a fusion of our physical, our digital, and our biological identities,"[29] an idea captured by the phrase "internet of bodies." "Recent technological advancements have ushered in a new era of the 'internet of bodies' (IoB)," states a 2020 WEF/McGill University briefing paper, "with an unprecedented number of connected devices and sensors being affixed to or even implanted and ingested into the human body. This has turned the human body into a technology platform. The IoB generates tremendous amounts of biometric and human behavioural data." Consider a future in which you are constantly connected to, and monitored by, global technology platforms.

The slide into this dystopian future has already begun through wearables and smart devices like Fitbits or Apple Watches, usually connected to digital applications, which track the most intimate aspects of our lives. Shoshana Zuboff chronicles many of these devices and their infractions, including smart beds that surreptitiously collect audio signals from your bedroom, and vacuum robots that calculate room and floor plan layouts of the homes they clean.[30] Anything advertised as "smart" is most likely sending incredible amount of personal, biometric, and/or household data back to the digital cloud. In these cases it is rarely clear how the data is or is not being used, and it can be insufferably difficult for a customer to "opt-out" of the surveillance collection of these devices, or even understand their "privacy" contracts in the first place.[31]

Implants are more problematic yet. Although uptake of elec-

---

29   Chicago Council on Global Affairs, "World Economic Forum Founder Klaus Schwab on the Fourth Industrial Revolution," *YouTube*, 2019, https://www.youtube.com/watch?v=CVIy3rjuKGY&t=960s.

30   Zuboff, *The Age of Surveillance Capitalism*, 234–37. For more on data collection from robot vacuums, see Eileen Guo, "A Roomba Recorded a Woman on the Toilet. How Did Screenshots End Up on Facebook?," MIT Technoloy Review, 2022, https://www.technologyreview.com/2022/12/19/1065306/roomba-irobot-robot-vacuums-artificial-intelligence-training-data-privacy/.

31   Zuboff, *The Age of Surveillance Capitalism*, 235–37.

tronically connected implants has so far been mostly limited to early adopters and medical patients, the surveillance-economy freight-train is barrelling towards what seems like its ultimate goal—every human digitally connected and surveilled.[32] Accenture and Microsoft have produced a persuasive video promoting a global digital ID program for the ID2020 Alliance. The presentation states that over 1.2 billion people live without proof of their identity, and it runs through a series of emotional scenarios facing the underprivileged: mobility issues, healthcare problems, etc. Having couched the argument in this language of human rights for the most vulnerable, the narrator provides the answer in a form of a question: "what if your identity was always in your hands?" as it shows the picture of the back of a human hand.[33] Implantable technology seems to be a particular interest of the Bill and Melinda Gates Foundation which has funded implantable birth-control microchips[34] and subcutaneous medical-information storage technology.[35]

Implant technology may soon extend to our minds as well. A WEF article by Kathleen Philips envisions digital augmentation, chip implants, and brain implants which may "allow us to tap straight into the body's 'operating system.'"[36] This technology is already available for medical patients, as in the example of an ALS patient who in December of 2021 sent a "telepathic" tweet using Synchron's brain

---

32   Alexandra Ma, "Thousands of People in Sweden Are Embedding Microchips Under Their Sking to Replace ID Cards," *Business Insider*, 2018, https://www.businessinsider.com/swedish-people-embed-microchips-under-skin-to-replace-id-cards-2018-5; Haley Weiss, "Why You're Probably Getting a Microchip Implant Someday," The Atlantic, 2018, https://www.theatlantic.com/technology/archive/2018/09/how-i-learned-to-stop-worrying-and-love-the-microchip/570946/.

33   Accenture Technology, "Establishing a Trusted Identity with Blockchain," *YouTube*, 2017, https://www.youtube.com/watch?v=r81Atqd2MM0&list=PLNop3ICb-Z4AX7_4ztH1MmTzFwbkkii6yf.

34   National Post Staff, "Bill Gates Funds Birth Control Microchip That Lasts 16 Years Inside the Body and Can Be Turned On or Off with Remote Control," *National Post*, 2014, https://nationalpost.com/news/bill-gates-funds-birth-control-microchip-that-lasts-16-years-inside-the-body-and-can-be-turned-on-or-off-with-remote-control.

35   Anne Trafton, "Storing Medical Information below the Skin's Surface," *MIT News*, 2019, https://news.mit.edu/2019/storing-vaccine-history-skin-1218.

36   Kathleen Philips, "Augmented Tech Can Change the Way We Live, but Only with the Right Support and Vision," *World Economic Forum*, 2022, https://www.weforum.org/agenda/2022/08/ethics-not-technological-limits-will-be-the-guiding-factor-for-an-augmented-age/.

interface.[37] Elon Musk, the innovator-billionaire behind Tesla and SpaceX, claims to be close to rolling out his brain-computer interface, Neuralink, and has applied to the FDA to begin human trials.[38] In a 2021 demonstration of the technology, a chimpanzee was able to play a simple video game with his mind alone.[39]

Given the pace of progress on brain-computer interfaces, and the startling advances in AI,[40] the future may not "merely" be one of constant digital surveillance, but one in which most of humanity is constantly connected to a global, digital intelligence which exhibits features of omniscience and omnipresence. Even at present, however, the realities of cancel culture, media suppression, vaccine passports, and China's social credit scoring system all suggest that a comprehensive social ostracization could be coming for those who will not bow to the world-system. If this is the case, it will not only be within the field of education that we need pioneering works. We may need an alternative culture.

We will need new ministries to the poor, the orphan, and the widow which will foresee opportunities for Christian love and the gospel within the devastation of a marginalizing culture, picking up the pieces after the Beast's pogrom. We will need new churches who will rally to the teaching and the testimony (Is 8:20) and bring in the harvest, if there is indeed at least one more great worldwide revival to come, as I argued at the end of the last chapter. We will need seminaries who will train men not only in conviction and competency, but also in courage, so that the church has leaders worth following in suffering for Christ's sake.

In a Beast-controlled, global ID future, we may also need

37   Joe Allen, "Hardwired for Control – The Brain-Computer Interface Is Already Here," *Singularity Weekly*, 2022, https://joebot.substack.com/p/hardwired-for-control-the-brain-computer?utm_source=profile&utm_medium=reader2.

38   "Elon Musk's Neuralink Brain Implant Could Begin Human Trials In 2023," *Forbes*, 2022, https://www.forbes.com/sites/qai/2022/12/07/elon-musks-neuralink-brain-implant-could-begin-human-trials-in-2023/?sh=2bb1e2f9147c.

39   Jane Wakefield, "Elon Musk's Neuralink 'Shows Monkey Playing Pong with Mind,'" *BBC News*, April 9, 2021, https://www.bbc.com/news/technology-56688812.

40   Nitasha Tiku, "The Google Engineer Who Thinks the Company's AI Has Come to Life," *Washington Post*, June 11, 2022, https://www.washingtonpost.com/technology/2022/06/11/google-ai-lamda-blake-lemoine/.

alternatives to public institutions and services which we currently take for granted. The time to build and prepare for this likely future is now. Healthcare facilities with the proper equipment need to be pioneered and staffed by medical practitioners who are not unduly influenced by pharmaceutical companies more intent on making money than on healing the sick.[41] This new crop of nurses and doctors ought to be trained and ready not only to minister to the body but also to the spirit through prayer and the Word, understanding that we are holistic persons and that sin has impacted both our flesh and our psyches.

As Martin Luther exhorted the councilmen of Germany in the time of the Reformation, libraries need to be built which will function as halls of true learning and house history's great books.[42] Many public libraries in North America are no more than liberal, secular-humanistic indoctrination centres, and are just as likely to promote a drag-queen story-time for children as a class which opens children's minds to the wonders of creation. We ought to build places of beauty, in which quiet contemplation away from the incessant noise and notifications of technology can take place in an environment of wood panelling, high rafters, and natural light. They do not need to be populated with every book on every subject. There is more than enough paper rubbish in the world already. Rather, a carefully curated collection, focusing on history, great literature, and timeless spiritual classics ought to form its foundation. "No expense should be spared" to accomplish this, Luther wrote.[43]

There is a great need for Christian trade schools as well. We have become a continent of specialists, and as the global economy has become more integrated, our Western specialties increasingly lie in white collar jobs and the service industry. We are in need of tradespeople and skilled labourers who know how to design, build, and develop. With greater breadth of skills will come greater independence from a paganized and increasingly controlling economic system. The trades

---

41   On the corruption of the pharmaceutical industry relative to mental illness, see Robert Whitaker, *Anatomy of an Epidemic* (New York: Broadway Books, 2010).

42   Luther, "To the Councilmen," 373–77.

43   Luther, "To the Councilmen," 373.

are often considered fields in which there is no obvious Christian perspective, but imagine a society in which Christian architects once again spurred each other on in glorifying God as they build edifices with great beauty according to harmonious and beautiful geometrical principles, as they did in the Gothic era. Envision a Christian fabricators guild which assumes that new innovations lie within their grasp as they pray for the creativity and insight to extend the dominion of man under Christ through the use of materials, metals, and machinery. Or a Christian research laboratory, where scientific breakthroughs outstrip secular discoveries by orders of magnitude as they build upon scriptural and creational presuppositions.

To these needs ought to be added entrepreneurship in business. Given the dominion mandate, is there anything more Christian than starting one's own business, trusting the Lord that He will provide as the entrepreneur labours and extends his reach? If the money earned is for God's glory in our families, churches, and society, who can doubt but that the Christian businessman ought to boldly claim promises like 2 Corinthians 8:8, "God is able to make all grace abound to you, so that having sufficiency in all things at all times, you may abound in every good work," or Isaiah 54:2, "Enlarge the place of your tent, and let the curtain of your habitations be stretched out; do not hold back; lengthen your cords and strengthen your stakes."

In whatever we pioneer, we must aim for excellence, so that not only will these ministries, institutions, and facilities suffice for their purposes, but so that they will be sought out by the world, *even as* they unashamedly hold to biblical principles and openly proclaim the truths of the gospel. It may be that we will once again see days like those of Solomon when the Queen of Sheba came from afar to see the success and wisdom granted to God's people (1 Kgs 10:1–10).

Venom and Victims

Sadly, what occurs so often in Christian organizations is the opposite. Instead of drawing unbelievers by how we conduct our affairs, including how God supplies abundantly for our needs, so many organizations import methods from the world, and rely upon government money and grants. This is a subtly dangerous relationship from which it may be almost impossible for an institution to extricate itself—the proverbial fly caught in the spiderweb.

It is a common misconception that spiderwebs are built in high-trafficked areas for the purpose of catching insects that happen to be flying by. Rather, spiderwebs are often built with particular characteristics, including non-structurally useful silk designs called "stabilimenta," which actively attract prey.[44] Moreover, recent research has demonstrated that when an insect gets close, spiderwebs spring towards insects due to "the electrostatic properties of the glue that coats spider webs" and the small electrical charges, whether positive or negative, that insects and other airborne substances carry.[45] Although Christian institutions face many dangers, the most deadly of them may be those which appear passive but are, in fact, purposefully predatory.

Free money is rarely free. It comes with subtle suppositions and crafty caveats which threaten Christian organizations; do not proselytize, do not talk about the supernatural, do not oppose our plans, do not engage in public debates on contentious issues. And slowly, the explicitly Christian ethos and foundation of the organization begins to wane, wrapped in the webbing of the world, starved without the constant sustenance of the Spirit-given Word, and obedience to it. Institutions may think they can cut off their relationship with the world and its capital at any time, but while they have taken the Beast's money, their budgets, capital projects, and salaries have grown increasingly reliant upon it, to the point where leaving the money becomes almost an impossibility, and envisions a death to the institution. It is this kind of context that breeds compromise.

How much better to heed the example of pioneers like George Müller, who in building orphanages for children in the nineteenth century, refused to even request money, and built on faith alone, trusting

---

44   James MacDonald, "Six Surprising Facts About Spiderwebs," *JSTOR Daily*, August 22, 2017, http://daily.jstor.org/surprising-facts-about-spiderwebs.

45   "How Electricity Helps Spider Webs Snatch Prey and Pollutants," *University of Oxford News*, December 2013, http://www.ox.ac.uk/news/2013-12-08-how-electricity-helps-spider-webs-snatch-prey-and-pollutants.

that God would supply. "In his mind," writes R. N. Shuff,

> the culture of the age was coloured by the scepticism of
> rational thought and scientific enquiry, which seemed to undermine
> the validity of orthodox Christianity's supernatural claims and led to
> a decline in popular belief. Müller's aim in founding an orphanage
> was to strengthen the faith of believers through "a visible proof" that
> God was still the same as in the past. Providing for the care of orphans
> through organized philanthropic activity would not meet this purpose.
> Only miraculous provision in direct response to prayer would arouse
> confidence in a living and personal God.[46]

God granted Müller success, and countless stories of God's
miraculous provision to Müller's orphanages have been told to the
glory of God.

Müller's approach is not the only faithful Christian model. I do
not believe that financial appeals or fundraising are inherently wrong.
But we ought to be exceedingly careful about building with capital
from the Beast-system. "Do not be unequally yoked with unbelievers,"
Paul warns, "For what partnership has righteousness with lawlessness?
Or what fellowship has light with darkness? What accord has Christ
with Belial?" (2 Cor 6:14–15).

PLUMB LINES

The prophet Amos ministered during the time of Uzziah, the great
builder-king of Judah, and his northern counterpart, Jeroboam II of
Israel (Amos 1:1). Using the metaphor of a plumb line to examine the
"building" of His people Israel, He declared a judgment of desolation
and destruction against them.

> This is what he showed me: behold, the Lord was standing
> beside a wall built with a plumb line, with a plumb line in his hand.
> And the LORD said to me, "Amos, what do you see?" And I said, "A
> plumb line." Then the Lord said, "Behold, I am setting a plumb line
> in the midst of my people Israel; I will never again pass by them; the

---

46   R. N. Shuff, "Müller, George," ed. Timothy Larsen et al., *Biographical Dictionary of Evangelicals* (Leicester, England; Downers Grove, IL: InterVarsity Press, 2003), 457.

high places of Isaac shall be made desolate, and the sanctuaries of Israel shall be laid waste, and I will rise against the house of Jeroboam with the sword." (Am 7:7–9)

In His Word, God has given us a blueprint for our pioneering architecture, whether it is of the sort that that is seen or unseen. If we do not build in the right way, or for the right reasons, we should expect that God will tear down and not build, pluck up and not plant. Pioneering the right way begins with building upon the foundation of Christ. He alone is a tested stone, a precious cornerstone, a sure foundation (Is 28:16). That "skilled master builder," the apostle Paul, exhorts,

> Let each one take care how he builds upon it. For no one can lay a foundation other than that which is laid, which is Jesus Christ. Now if anyone builds on the foundation with gold, silver, precious stones, wood, hay, straw— each one's work will become manifest, for the Day will disclose it, because it will be revealed by fire, and the fire will test what sort of work each one has done. (1 Cor 3:10–13)

In the greater context of 1 Corinthians, this means a focus on "Jesus Christ and him crucified" (1 Cor 2:2) and putting away the world's methods and "wisdom" for how to build (1 Cor 2:4–6).[47] Whatever we build for the glory of God, there ought to be an explicit and regularly communicated commitment to God's Word and His laws. Those who are employed by, or connected with, our works, ought to regularly hear the Word of Christ being spoken, prayed, and even preached. Of course, this will look different depending on what we are building, whether we are planting a church or pioneering a Christ-honoring health clinic. Nevertheless, everything begins and ends with the Word of God.

We also ought to consider our motivation for pioneering. There is a justified thrill in a new project—those first steps into the unknown, the exploration of a new frontier, or the initiation of a never-before attempted endeavour. It is the nature of man, creationally, to build. It is also the nature of man, creationally, to succeed. But outward success

---

47   Paul is speaking about the church, but the principles here may be readily applied to other Christian endeavours.

may not last long if the motivation is not the glory of God.

The Tower of Babel stands as an important warning. The motive of the builders was idolatrous—to make a name for themselves (Gn 10:4). In light of this, it is remarkable that as He observed the progress of their project, the Lord stated "this is only the beginning of what they will do. And nothing that they propose to do will now be impossible for them" (Gn 10:6). As noted earlier, God finally intervened, but not before leaving us with wisdom and a warning concerning the creational abilities of man. Our projects may seem to work and to succeed for some time. However, if the work is not for the purpose of glorifying God, and is instead about making a name or a kingdom for ourselves, in the end the work will fail, or as the apostle Paul states, burn (1 Cor 3:13).

The plumb line of God will pass over every one of our works. Will it endure to Christ's glory and our reward?

A Workforce for Broken Walls

Nehemiah is one of the great builders in the Bible. God called him out of the court of the Persian king, as I've suggested probably Darius the Great,[48] to aid the returned exiles of Jerusalem in rebuilding its walls. Although a gifted, strong, and experienced leader, he knew well that the enormous work of repairing the walls required a great workforce—he could not begin do it alone.

Nehemiah chapter 3 is a chronicle of the workers and their parts in the corporate effort. At first glance it may look like a record of unpronounceable names and unfamiliar locations in a repetitive narrative. But sustained study yields significant insights. Some "great" men thought the work below them (v5). Those with unique skills were willing to do hard labour outside their specialties (v8). Some families repaired more than one section (v5, 27). And in at least one case, women joined the men in the hard manual labour (v12). Above all, the

---

48   James B. Jordan, "Esther: Historical & Chronological Comments (III),"
Biblical Chronology 8, no. 5 (1996), http://www.biblicalhorizons.com/biblical-chronology/8_05/.

chapter illustrates the need for partners and co-workers in the building program of God.

The picture of the "pioneer" conjures up images of the poor family standing outside their sod-house with no one within a dozen miles—alone, bereft, squalid. Although there are times and places in which a pioneering work may begin in isolation, most of the time the Lord provides partners and co-labourers for the work. We may feel like we have to take a step out into uncharted waters, but even as we do, we will often find that the Spirit has moved other saints to take that same step at precisely the same time.

The apostle Paul was one of the most gifted leaders and pioneers the world has ever seen, and yet even he had his apostolic band— co-workers in the great building project of the Gentile church. He was a planter, but others came shortly after to water (1 Cor 3:6). And when he was alone, he was restless (2 Cor 2:13), perhaps knowing that the normative procedure for pioneering is to go out two by two (Lk 10:1).

If the Lord leads you to start some new work, look for others that the Spirit may be simultaneously prompting in the same direction. I have experienced this myself in new educational projects begun here in Greater Vancouver. I vividly remember the day that several parents met together to think about what was next for a cohort of classically homeschooled high-school graduates. The idea, bolstered by past conversation about the need for a robustly Christian Bible college in the area which focused on worldview, apologetics, and the liberal arts, came clearly to my mind that this was the time to initiate something. But how to proceed with such an enormous undertaking? A day later I received an email from a fellow pastor at our church with a background in education— "the Lord has been speaking to me about doubling-down on our educational emphasis. What might this look like?" Later that week, when I told him what the Spirit had put upon my own heart through the prior meeting, his response confirmed clearly that we needed to pioneer a new liberal arts college immediately.

Labouring alongside others greatly increases the joy of the work. There is a blessed fellowship and camaraderie as both victories and struggles are shared, prayed about, and built upon. "Two are better than one," says the Teacher, "because they have a good reward for their toil" (Ec 4:9). But as we have already considered, there is also an element of battle to our building projects. The devil and the Beast-system of the world will do what they can to interrupt or even tear down the work of God. This is clearly seen in the story of Nehemiah. Two major antagonists, Tobiah and Sanballat, opposed the rebuilding of Jerusalem's walls and conspired against the Jews at every turn. At one point the danger was so great that the labourers had to carry on the construction with one hand while holding a sword in the other (Neh 4:17). If the work of construction is benefitted by at least two working side by side, how much more when it incorporates an aspect of warfare? "And though a man might prevail against one who is alone, two will withstand him—a threefold cord is not quickly broken" (Ec 4:12).

THE MACHINERY OF FAITH

The story of Christian businessman R.G. LeTourneau holds a special place in my heart. It was the first Christian book my father ever read when he came to faith in Christ through the ministry of a pioneering church planter in Squamish, BC. In his autobiography, *Mover of Men and Mountains*, LeTourneau chronicles his adventures as a Christian businessman and inventor who built enormous land-movers and revolutionized large-scale projects in the United States. During the difficult years of the Great Depression, LeTourneau's manufacturing business was blessed by God. In 1932, his yearly net profit was $52,000; in 1934 it ballooned to $340,000, and by 1938 it was a staggering $1.4 million, which amounts to almost $30 million today.[49]

What was R.G.'s secret? The Lord gifted him with an engineer's mind, an adventurous streak, and an incredible work ethic. But it was his commitment to the Lord as his business partner that he emphasized whenever he had the opportunity to speak on the subject. In 1935, as the business began to take off, he and his wife Evelyn committed to

---

49   "RG LeTourneau - Earthmoving Innovator," *Giants for God*, n.d., http://www.giantsforgod.com/rg-letourneau/.

a tithe of their profits—to themselves! Ninety percent went to the Lord. "If there is no logical explanation of my development of the digger," he reflects in the introduction of his book, "there is a theological one, available to all of us, including the weakest. By accepting God as your partner, no limit can be placed on what can be achieved."[50]

Joe Boot agrees that when God and His glory is the vision of pioneering projects, supply and support will never lack.[51] Boot had been speaking and traveling widely as an apologist in the 2000s, when he noticed that the questions people were asking about the Christian faith and worldview were changing drastically. It was no longer "does God exist?" or "did Christ really rise from the dead?", but "is Christianity homophobic?" and "does the Bible teach colonialism?" This led Boot to pioneer a cultural apologetics ministry and think tank in Canada, the Ezra Institute, and then to plant a church and classical school where all of this reflection and thinking could be put to the test—in downtown Toronto, an "inner-city, pagan environment."

Boot's vision of God's kingdom as a comprehensive reality that is not restricted to personal salvation, together with the belief that culture always reflects society's beliefs, meant for this pioneer that institutions had to be built. Boot believes that the Western church is currently at "an inflection point."

> We have been living on the fumes of the faith of our forefathers. Because we have not given ourselves as Christians, for the most part, to the concrete applications of our faith in culture, and to the building of institutions, our cultural capital has been so depleted that our influence has been radically reduced. Furthermore, the marvellous institutions our forebears built have now been taken over by another faith. They have been captured by humanism and new-paganism and are now destroying the fabric of our society.

At this "epochal turning point," Boot reflects, "either the Western church will recapture a culture-building mandate or it will fade away until it is renewed by a missionary movement from the develop-

---

50   R. G. LeTourneau, *Mover of Men and Mountains* (Chicago: Moody Press, 1972), 3.

51   The following account and details are taken from a personal interview with the author February 3, 2022.

ing world."

Boot is no pessimist, however. He believes in God's promises to build His kingdom, and in bold faith as the right response to them. God has blessed his approach in many ways, granting him success in his pioneering efforts, and supplying their ministries abundantly. "I have never done fund-raising," Boot remarks upon God's supply, "but we have received many millions of dollars in donations of money and real-estate because people believe in our theological vision."

His testimony reminds me of the famous saying of William Carey, early Baptist missionary to India, "expect great things from God, attempt great things for God." Boot has adopted Douglas Wilson's similar, simpler, phrase : "Geronimo, Amen."

So, go build something. The Lord is with you. Practice pioneering.

APOCALYPSE-PREPARATION LIST

- Take stock of your expertise and interests. What can you build that will contribute to God-glorifying dominion?
- Learn new skills that expand your repertoire of usefulness for Christ, your family, and the church.
- Resolve to never take part in a global digital identity program or to implant a technological device that will permit your surveillance. Be cautious even with "smart" devices, smartphones, and wearables.
- Build in such a way that you are independent from government money, and fully free to pursue your project in ways that would most honor Christ.
- Pray for God to reveal co-workers who have a similar vision in pioneering.
- Make the Lord your business partner, and honor Him with the first-fruits of all your blessings of influence, success, and riches.
- Attempt something and step out in faith!
- Memorize 1 Corinthians 3:10–15. "According to the grace of God given to me, like a skilled master builder I laid a foundation, and someone else is building upon it. Let each one take care how he builds upon it. For no one can lay a foundation other than that which is laid, which is Jesus Christ. Now if anyone builds on the foundation with gold, silver, precious stones, wood, hay, straw— each one's work will become manifest, for the Day will disclose it, because it will be revealed by fire, and the fire will test what sort of work each one has done. If the work that anyone has built on the foundation survives, he will receive a reward. If anyone's work is burned up, he will suffer loss, though he himself will be saved, but only as through fire."

CHAPTER 6

Don't Dine with Demons

THE DEMONIC CONSPIRACY

In 586 BC, Nebuchadnezzar and his general, Nebuzaradan, conquered Jerusalem and carried away its citizens into exile, leaving in Judah only the poorest (Jer 40:7), the princesses (Jer 43:6), and the eunuchs (Jer 41:16). The man he left in charge, however, was a sincere and capable man by the name of Gedaliah. A well-respected leader, when the guerilla troops which were left in the open country heard of his appointment, they rallied to him (Jer 40:7). Gedaliah reminded them of the word of Jeremiah, that God would bless them as they served the King of Babylon (v9), and he vowed to represent them to Babylon from Mizpah, a welcome promise for those who had recently been openly hostile to their conquerors (v10). Judean refugees who had previously fled to Moab, Edom, and elsewhere, likewise returned to Mizpah under Gedaliah's leadership and in that year "gathered wine and summer fruits in great abundance" (v12).

It seemed as if God's favour was on the early governorship of Gedaliah but, as one commentator notes, "evil spirits were at work against him."[1] A troubling rumour arose from within his own cabinet. Johanan, the son of Kareah, came secretly to the governor with a serious accusation: one of their council, Ishmael the son of Nethaniah, was secretly working for Baalis, king of the Ammonites, and was planning to murder him (v13–14). Gedaliah didn't believe the conspiracy theory.

---

1   James Crichton, "Gedaliah," in *The International Standard Bible Encyclopaedia* (The Howard-Severance Company, 1915).

Johanan pressed him, offering to personally strike Ishmael down—why should their early success be jeopardized (v15)? But the governor was unmoved. Perhaps he even wondered if Johanan had a personal vendetta against his compeer, reproving him: "You shall not do this thing, for you are speaking falsely of Ishmael" (v16).

A short while later, Gedaliah was at the supper table with Ishmael and ten of his men when they rose up and murdered the promising figure and all those associated with him at Mizpah (Jer 41:1–3). The event threw the already vulnerable nation into a tailspin, eventually leading to their flagrantly disobedient pilgrimage to Egypt. The conspiracy was real.

It ought to be noted that there are occasions in which the prophets warn against the swirling winds of conspiracy, as when Isaiah warned in the days of Ahaz, "Do not call conspiracy all that this people calls conspiracy, and do not fear what they fear, nor be in dread" (Is 8:12). But there are other times in which God gives knowledge and insight to his people to see the hidden plots which threaten them. Nehemiah had the wisdom to see the hostility and conspiratorial intent of Tobiah and Sanballat (Neh 6:1–14). Esther and Mordecai worked together to reverse the murderous conspiracy of Haman against the Jewish people dwelling in Persia's realms. The son of Paul's sister overheard the oath of forty Jewish men in their plot to kill the apostle and it was God's providence that the centurion and tribune believed the young man (Acts 23:12–22). Chief of all conspiracies was the plot of the Jewish leaders to "arrest Jesus by stealth and kill him" (Mt 26:4), a scheme that was put into action when the devil himself entered Judas to finalize the betrayal of Christ (Lk 22:3–6).

It is common to dismiss those who warn of apocalyptic trajectories or patterns in our day by naming them "conspiracy theorists." But it is naïve to dismiss the idea of conspiracy with a wave of the hand given what Scripture reveals of the purposes of evil powers. It is clear in the book of Daniel that spiritual powers fight against the purposes of God (Dn 10:13), and Psalm 2 states that "the nations rage and the peoples plot in vain...against the Lord and against his Anointed" (Ps 2:1–2).

In times of apocalypse, the machinations and stratagems of demons and wicked rulers erupt in malevolent "successes" that threaten truth, goodness, and freedom. Less than one year before Hitler assumed power in Germany as chancellor, Dietrich Bonhoeffer stated in his lecture, "The Church is Dead,"

> How can one close one's eyes at the fact that the demons themselves have taken over the rule of the world, that it is the powers of darkness who have here made an awful conspiracy and could break out at any moment? —How could one think that these demons could be driven out, these powers annihilated with a bit of education in international understanding, with a bit of goodwill?[2]

In considering the sins and depravity of our current world and its leaders, it once again seems as if the demons have conspired to take over the rule of the world. One Christian may believe in more conspiracy theories, and another in less. But regardless of the specifics of said theories, what is an utter and complete failure of theology is the trust of many Christians in the basic morality or good intentions of unbelieving leaders and governments. Joseph Exell, reflecting on the prophecy that Babylon will become "a dwelling place for demons, a haunt for every unclean spirit" (Rv 18:2), concludes,

> Such is the appointed end of every political or religious system that ignores God and His truth, and seek [sic] after material power and prosperity as the chief objects of life. Let a nation lose her faith in God—let her drive truth, virtue, love, and righteousness from her heart and life, and what will she become? Can she become anything else than a habitation of devils? Can she become anything else but the seat and prey of demon-like passions?[3]

In this chapter we will consider the evils of the current world system and its leaders, what they portend of future abominations, and how the saints can and must escape complicity in these evils. You must "come out of her [Babylon], lest you take part in her sins, lest you

---

2   Lecture delivered August 29, 1932. Originally from *A Testament to Freedom: The Essential Writings of Dietrich Bonhoeffer*, cited here from Robert Ewusie Moses, "Powerful Practices: Paul's Principalities and Powers Revisited" (Duke University, 2012), https://dukespace.lib.duke.edu/dspace/bitstream/handle/10161/5731/.

3   Joseph S. Exell, *The Biblical Illustrator: Revelation* (London: James Nisbet and Co., n.d.), 534.

share in her plagues; for her sins are heaped high as heaven, and God has remembered her iniquities" (Rv 18:4–5). For the sake of brevity, we will focus on three areas of evil, arguably the three greatest sins: murder, sexual immorality, and idolatry.[4]

BLOOD ON YOUR HANDS

Although the extensive warfare and death which characterized the 20th century has come to an end, murder is more common now than ever. As it states of Babylon in Revelation 18:24, "in her was found the blood…of all who have been slain on earth."[5] As of 2022, over 63 million pre-born babies have been killed through abortion in the United States alone.[6] Infants ripped limb from limb within their mother's womb,[7] the virtual extermination of Down's syndrome persons in many nations,[8] women with mental health issues caused by guilt,[9] and a black population in the US significantly suppressed by prenatal murder:[10] the repercussions of widespread abortion are simultaneously

---

4   These three evils are listed in almost every sin list in the Scriptures, and are often present even in a list of two or three representative or heinous sins (Eph 5:5, Rv 22:15).

5   Within the category of murder, the emphasis in Revelation is on martyrdom and the death of the saints. Although we see persecution and martyrdom of Christians currently in the world, and world leaders often turn a blind-eye to it and its extent (see Bishop Truro's report below), because it has not risen yet to a global level or policy-level, I have decided to focus on those aspects of murder—abortion and euthanasia—which have. For more on Christian persecution, see Philip Mountstephen, "Bishop of Truro's Independent Review for the Foreign Secretary of FCO Support for Persecuted Christians: Final Report and Recommendations," 2019, https://christianpersecutionreview.org.uk/report/.

6   Live Action, "Learn About the Problem," 2022, https://www.liveaction.org/learn/the-problem/.

7   Choice42, "The Procedure," *YouTube*, 2022, https://www.youtube.com/watch?v=nd_9y1-L60c.

8   Evita Duffy, "It Is Not 'Humane' For The Atlantic To Sympathize With Killing Babies With Down Syndrome, Like My Little Sister," *The Federalist*, 2020, https://thefederalist.com/2020/11/30/it-is-not-humane-for-the-atlantic-to-sympathize-with-killing-babies-with-down-syndrome-like-my-little-sister/.

9   For an overview of the abortion and mental health studies, see David C Reardon, "The Abortion and Mental Health Controversy : A Comprehensive Liiterature Review of Common Ground Agreements , Disagreements , Actionable Recommendations , and Research Opportunities," *SAGE Open Medicine* 6 (2018): 1–38, https://doi.org/10.1177/2050312118807624.

10   Arthur Goldberg, "Abortion's Devastating Impact Upon Black Americans," *The Public Discourse*, 2019, https://www.thepublicdiscourse.com/2019/02/48594/.

comprehensive and incomprehensible. And so, the June 2022 Supreme Court overturning of Roe v. Wade hails as one of the most significant victories for justice in recent decades. The response from major world leaders and organizations, however, was swift and virtually universal in its condemnation of the decision. UN High Commissioner for Human Rights Michelle Bachelet stated, "Access to safe, legal and effective abortion is firmly rooted in international human rights law and is at the core of women and girls' autonomy and ability to make their own choices about their bodies and lives, free of discrimination, violence and coercion."[11]

Although pro-life advocates in the United States are rightly celebrating this recent victory, world organizations such as the UN, UNICEF, WHO have been quietly but powerfully strengthening the practice of abortion through the proliferation of policies that connect it to various rights: women's rights, health rights, sexual rights, and more. Framed in this way, those on the left have increasingly, and in some cases radically, moved from the opinion that "abortion should be safe, legal, and rare," a phrase used by Bill Clinton in the early '90s.[12] In spite of the fact that babies beyond 20 weeks can survive outside of the womb, and feel pain,[13] many American Democrats, including Raphael Warnock, John Fetterman, and President Joe Biden, refuse to support any limit on abortion whatsoever.[14]

In Canada, the situation is even worse. Without any law or limits on abortion since the 1988 *Morgentaler* Supreme Court decision, Canada is the only democracy in the world without legal protections for the pre-born.[15] This means that it is legal to abort a baby at 39 or 40

---

11   Zoe Christen Jones, "World Leaders React to the U.S. Supreme Court's Decision to Overturn Roe v. Wade," *CBS News*, 2022, https://www.cbsnews.com/news/supreme-court-roe-v-wade-abortion-rights-international-response/.

12   Anna North, "How the Abortion Debate Moved Away from 'Safe, Legal, and Rare,'" *Vox*, 2019, https://www.vox.com/2019/10/18/20917406/abortion-safe-legal-and-rare-tulsi-gabbard.

13   Steven Ertelt, "Fetal Anesthesia Expert: Unborn Children Feel Pain, Even Before Viability," *LifeNews*, 2013, https://www.lifenews.com/2013/09/03/fetal-anesthesia-expert-unborn-children-feel-pain-even-before-viability/.

14   The Editors, "Democrats Double-Down on Abortion Extremism," *National Review*, 2022, https://www.nationalreview.com/2022/10/democrats-double-down-on-abortion-extremism/.

15   Anna Nienhuis, "January 28 Marks Thirty-Four Years of No Abortion Law

weeks. Pro-choice advocates argue that this rarely happens. However, data uncovered by Freedom of Information requests reveal that not only do late-term abortions occur in Canada, but more heinous evils yet are being perpetrated.[16] According to statistics obtained from the Canadian Institute of Health Information by pro-life advocate Patricia Maloney, there were 127 live-birth abortions in 2020/2021.[17] These represent attempts to kill a late-term baby in which the child originally survives the abortion and is born alive before being abandoned to die outside the womb.[18] Consider that *hundreds* of infanticides have taken place in the last several years in this "advanced" democracy.

Recently, Canada has also expanded the range of eligible criteria under which a person can access Medical Assistance in Dying (MAiD), a euphemism for suicide aided by a medical professional. Only six years ago Canada permitted euthanasia for a very small group of people whose deaths were imminent. The slippery slope has been a very steep one. Starting in March 2024, euthanasia will be permitted for mental illness. Those with experiences as subjective as depression, loneliness, and feeling unloved, will apply, and may very well be approved, for the procedure. The government has also been considering extending MAiD to "mature minors" under 18 years of age,[19] and the

in Canada," *We Need a Law*, 2022, https://weneedalaw.ca/press-release/press-release-january-28-marks-34-years-of-no-abortion-law-in-canada/.

16   The Canadian Institute for Health Information reports that for 2017 (excluding Quebec) 3.2% (706) of the total reported induced abortions were at 21 weeks gestation or more. However, fully 19.2% of total abortions had "unknown" gestational age. Of those abortions with known gestational age, 4% were at 21 weeks or more. Another 5.1% were at 17 to 20 weeks. Some pro-life advocates suggest that abortions are not fully reported. This would seem corroborated by comparing the subsequent statistics on live-birth abortions with the CIHI data on late-term abortions. With the caveats of comparing 2022 and 2017 figures, the exclusion of Quebec totals, and other omissions across Canada, it seems inconceivable that abortion doctors could botch these abortion procedures at a ratio of anything remotely close to 1:7. It would seem a safe assumption, therefore, that the true number of yearly late-term abortions in Canada is significantly larger than the 706 reported in the 2017 CIHI data, perhaps by an order of magnitude. "Induced Abortions Reported in Canada in 2017," Canadian Institute for Health Information, 2017, https://www.cihi.ca/en/induced-abortions-reported-in-canada-in-2017.

17   Anna Nienhuis, "Live-Birth Abortion Numbers Increase in Canada," *ARPA Canada*, 2022, https://weneedalaw.ca/2022/06/live-birth-abortion-numbers-increase-in-canada/.

18   Nienhuis, "Live-Birth Abortion Numbers Increase".

19   Irene Grace Bom, "Bereaved Canadian Parents Call for Better Palliative Care Instead of Assisted Suicide," *Lifesite*, 2022, https://www.lifesitenews.com/news/

increasing acceptance of euthanasia within a state-run health system means that, increasingly, patients with long-term disabilities will be offered euthanasia as the "solution" to their problems.

This is already taking place, as recent hearings in the Canadian Parliament conclusively demonstrate that Armed Force veterans are being offered MAiD if they are suffering—in many cases from injuries or trauma directly related to their service![20] "If it's too difficult for you to continue living, Madam," read one letter, "we can offer you medical assistance in dying,"[21] Tim Stainton, director of the Canadian Institute for Inclusion and Citizenship at the University of British Columbia, states that Canadian law is "probably the biggest existential threat to disabled people since the Nazis' program in Germany in the 1930s."[22]

Death is not only being normalized in Western society, it is being celebrated and glamorized. A recent advertisement by Canadian fashion company Simons is a case in point. Their three-minute film titled "All is Beauty," set to moving scenes of the ocean, music-making, and a dinner party, describes "the most beautiful exit" of a young woman who was euthanized only days after the footage was taken.[23] For years she had sought treatment for Ehlers-Danlos syndrome, "a rare and painful condition in which patients suffer from excessively fragile skin and connective issues."[24] However, her decision to undergo euthanasia seemed significantly related to her inability to find proper treatment for her condition. "I feel like I'm falling through the cracks" she stated in a television interview earlier that year, "so if I'm not able

bereaved-canadian-parents-call-for-better-palliative-care-over-assisted-suicide/.

20   Michael Higgins, "Michael Higgins: Our Veterans Ask for Help. They're Offered Assisted Death," *National Post*, December 2, 2022, https://nationalpost.com/opinion/our-veterans-ask-for-help-theyre-offered-assisted-death.

21   Higgins, " Our Veterans Ask for Help."

22   Gus Alexiou, "Canada's New Euthanasia Laws Carry Upsetting Nazi-Era Echoes, Warns Expert," *Forbes*, August 15, 2022, https://www.forbes.com/sites/gusalexiou/2022/08/15/canadas-new-euthanasia-laws-carry-upsetting-nazi-era-echoes-warns-expert/?sh=2244de1ac7b8.

23   Simons, "All Is Beauty," *YouTube*, 2022, https://www.youtube.com/watch?v=dCafuU5CCfA.

24   Tristin Hopper, "Woman Featured in Pro-Euthanasia Commercial Wanted to Live, Say Friends," *National Post*, December 5, 2022, https://nationalpost.com/news/canada/woman-euthanasia-commercial-wanted-to-live.

to access health care am I then able to access death care?'"[25] The answer, increasingly, is "yes," to the most vulnerable in society. And not only are these deaths occurring, they are being romanticized.

Abortion, too, has been recently and similarly celebrated. The "Shout Your Abortion" campaign which started in 2015 gained new life in 2022 as a response to the Roe v. Wade decision. Movement co-founder Lindy West wrote at its inception, "Plenty of people still believe that on some level – if you are a good woman – abortion is a choice which should be accompanied by some level of sadness, shame or regret. But you know what? I have a good heart and having an abortion made me happy in a totally unqualified way."[26] Singer Lily Allen wrote more recently on Instagram, "I wish people would stop posting examples of exceptional reasons for having abortions. Most people I know, myself included, just didn't want to have a f---ing baby. AND THAT IS REASON ENOUGH! WE DON'T HAVE TO JUSTIFY IT."

It is clear that the devil is not satisfied simply with more death. He wants a *religion* of death, a world in which death is not seen as "the last enemy to be destroyed" (1 Cor 15:26), but a celebrated means of ultimate autonomy from the Creator and Sustainer of life. He hates all ten of God's laws, and wants to relegate the first law of the second table— "do not murder"—to a bygone age.

THE SLIDE TO SODOM

Another major indictment of the harlot in Revelation is sexual immorality. "For all nations have drunk the wine of the passion of her sexual immorality, and the kings of the earth have committed immorality with her" (Rv 18:3). As the symbolic paragon of paganism, Babylon stands in a long line of nations, like Sodom and Canaan, given over to debauchery. Since the sexual revolution of the 1960s, there has been a steady growth in the acceptance and celebration of increasingly de-

---

25   Hopper "Woman Featured."

26   Lindy West, "I Set Up #ShoutYourAbortion Because I Am Not Sorry, and I Will Not Whisper," The Guardian, 2015, https://www.theguardian.com/commentis-free/2015/sep/22/i-set-up-shoutyourabortion-because-i-am-not-sorry-and-i-will-not-whisper.

grading sexual practices. Depravity has been mainstreamed.

Cross-dressers, drag-queens, and fetishists openly parade their licentiousness in the upper echelons of society. Carl Trueman writes that Joe Biden's appointment of cross-dressing queer advocate Sam Brinton to the U.S. Department of Energy is "the latest sign of decadence in the dying culture of the West."[27] Although Trueman notes that so exotic and public are his perversions that he cannot in good conscience describe them in the article, Rod Dreher reports with some detail on Brinton's very public advocacy for kinks like sodomy, domination, masochism, and "puppy-play," which steers into mock-bestiality.[28] As another example, US Army colonel, Brian T. Connelly has been open about his puppy-play fetish, wearing his uniform with his pup-fetish-mask on social media posts, and openly engaging in his perverse behaviour with a subordinate officer.[29] "When our New Woke Military celebrates Pride, do they mean Pup Pride too?," Dreher asks, "If not, why not? What are the boundaries for the military in tolerating this filth?"[30]

There are not many outrageous acts left for the new pagans to normalize. Polyamory, "open relationships," and swinging are all mostly accepted. The *Fifty Shades of Grey* series has normalized sadomasochism. Choking, now a regular part of online pornography, is being practiced by more and more young men during intercourse who have learned sexual behavior through online porn consumption.[31] And the shame of incest is being slowly eroded by the mainstream media through shows like *Game of Thrones*. "If there is one peculiar achievement that is testament to the all-conquering cultural influence

27   Carl R. Trueman, "Decadence on Display," *World*, February 21, 2022, https://wng.org/opinions/decadence-on-display-1645449344.

28   Trueman; Rod Dreher, "Biden Puttin' On the Dog," *The American Conservative*, 2022, https://www.theamericanconservative.com/sam-brinton-kinky-joe-biden-puttin-on-the-dog/.

29   Rod Dreher, "US Military Going To The Dogs," *The American Conservative*, 2022, https://www.theamericanconservative.com/us-military-going-to-the-dogs/.

30   Dreher, "US Military."

31   Olga Khazan, "How Porn Is Affecting Choking During Sex," *The Atlantic*, June 24, 2019, https://www.theatlantic.com/health/archive/2019/06/how-porn-affecting-choking-during-sex/592375/. The presentation of the "solutions" in this article are almost as shocking as the problems it unearths.

of HBO's *Game of Thrones*," writes Tony Wong in the *Toronto Star*, "it is that they managed to get viewers rooting for incest."[32] Pedophilia is one of the only taboos left, but perhaps not for much longer.

The July 2019 arrest of billionaire Jeffery Epstein brought the idea of global-elite child sex-trafficking out of the shadows of internet rumours into the light of day. His subsequent death in jail under suspicious circumstances,[33] his connection to Prince Albert who settled a lawsuit with rape-accuser Virginia Giuffre,[34] and the failure of authorities to shut down the operation much earlier,[35] have not quelled public rumblings that much more lies hidden underneath the surface. In addition to these troubling suspicions, the sheer volume and almost exponential growth of child pornography on the Internet suggests that child sexual abuse may be highly prevalent.[36]

In November of 2022, a public scandal hit fashion designer Balenciaga for its child BDSM-themed photoshoot not only sexualizing children, but involving them in violent, abusive themes. In a short article for *The American Conservative*, Rod Dreher drew the conclusion obvious to anyone willing to consider the evidence; someone at Balenciaga deliberately used the photoshoot to push a grotesque child-sexual abuse message. There were plush animals dressed in BDSM clothing, a partially hidden file folder with legal documents from a child-sex court case, and a roll of caution-tape that read "Baalenciaga" instead of "Balenciaga."[37]

---

32   Tony Wong, "How Game of Thrones Got Us to Root for Incest and Other Debauchery," *Toronto Star*, April 8, 2019, https://www.thestar.com/entertainment/opinion/2019/04/08/how-game-of-thrones-got-us-to-root-for-incest-and-other-debauchery.html.

33   Luke Barr, "More Questions than Answers 2 Years After Epstein's Suicide," *ABC News*, August 11, 2021, https://abcnews.go.com/US/questions-answers-years-epsteins-suicide/story?id=79379998.

34   Caroline Downey, "Prince Andrew Settles with Accuser Virginia Giuffre in Sexual Abuse Lawsuit," *National Review*, 2022, https://www.nationalreview.com/news/prince-andrew-settles-with-accuser-virginia-giuffre-in-sexual-abuse-lawsuit/.

35   Andrew Anthony, "Meet Julie K Brown, the Woman Who Brought Down Jeffrey Epstein," *The Guardian*, July 25, 2021, https://www.theguardian.com/us-news/2021/jul/25/meet-julie-k-brown-the-woman-who-brought-down-jeffrey-epstein.

36   "2021 Annual Report: Total Number of Reports," *Internet Watch Foundation*, 2021, https://annualreport2021.iwf.org.uk/trends/total.

37   Rod Dreher, "Balenciaga: Child Sacrifice, Cannibalism, & Couture," *The American Conservative*, 2022, https://www.theamericanconservative.com/balenciaga-child-sacrifice-cannibalism-couture/.

A concurrent photo shoot by the fashion line included highly disturbing books, such as *Fire From the Sun* by Michael Borremans, which contains depictions of nude children and body parts covered in blood. "Do you want to know why Jeffrey Epstein was still celebrated by the rich and famous, even after he was convicted of sex with minors?" Dreher asks in conclusion, "There's probably a connection between that and what Balenciaga has done here. Among the super-rich, this stuff is normal."[38] Only the most charitable (or naïve) interpretation of the evidence could come to a different conclusion.

The West's remaining sexual taboos—bestiality, incest, and pedophilia—remain such only on account of two principles: consent and harm. If it can be demonstrated that any or all of these practices are consensual and not harmful, these evils will be celebrated just as openly as anything else taking place currently at Pride parades. Most people are unaware, however, just how thin are the threads providing this restraint in the world's man-centered "religion."

Take pedophilia, for example. In regard to consent, there is a worldwide push to grant children "sexual rights or "sexual agency." Often under the guise of preparing children for sexual practices already taking place among their peers, or preventing child marriage, children are increasingly being regarded as sexual beings with sexual autonomy, and at ever-decreasing or ambiguous ages. A 2022 UNICEF paper states, "Ensuring the minimum age of consent to sex is consistent with the onset of consensual sexual activity in adolescents recognizes and protects young people's agency to engage in consensual relationships.[39]

Within the peer-reviewed literature there are many examples of viewing adolescents or children as sexually autonomous, often in connection with LGBT ideology. One example, which also undermines the idea of pedophilic harm, is Carballo-Dieguez's "Recalled Sexual Ex-

---

38   Dreher. See the subsequent section on occultism as well, as child sexual abuse and Satanism often seem to be linked.

39   United Nations Children's Fund and United Naitons Population Fund, *Beyond Marriage and Motherhood: Empowering Girls by Addressing Adolescent Pregnancies, Child Marriages and Early Unions – Tailoring Programme Interventions for Southeast Asia and the Pacific.* (Bangkok: UNICEF East Asia and Pacific Regional Office, 2022), https://www.unicef.org/eap/media/11031/file/Beyond Marriage and Motherhood - Tailoring Programme Interventions.pdf.

periences in Childhood with Older Partners," in which he reports that in a study of 575 gay males and transgender male-to-females in Brazil, 32% of the sample reported childhood sexual experiences with an older partner.[40] Of this group, the mean age at first experience was 9 years, and their "partners" (the language used in the study) were, on average, 19 years old. Appallingly "only 29% of the participants who had had such childhood sexual experiences considered it abuse," and "57% reported liking" the experience.[41] "Results highlight the importance of assessing participants' perception of abuse," the authors write, "regardless of researchers' pre-determined criteria to identify abuse."[42] Although it is couched in academic language, the underlying conclusion here is chilling. Is it abuse if the child enjoys the sexual act? Is it harmful if they look back upon it as a positive experience?

The rainbow is often used as a Trojan horse to sexualize children in our culture. Here in the BC education system, LGBT advocates have been active in crafting a sex and gender program that is woven throughout the entire province's approach to education and curriculum.[43] There are approved BC Teacher's Federation lesson plans in which Kindergartners are taught about masturbation and directed to draw and name male and female genitalia on blank figures.[44] This instruction is under the pretense of protection and teaching children consent. In the later years, the disguise is not nearly as complete. Rainbow-themed books found in the school system include graphic illustrations of cunnilingus, masturbation, adolescent gay sex, and at least in one case, an illustration of child-sex conduct/abuse.[45]

---

40   Alex Carballo-Dieguez, "Recalled Sexual Experiences in Childhood with Older Partners : A Study of Brazilian Men Who Have Sex with Men Abd Male-to-Female Transgender Persons," *Archives of Sexual Behavior*, no. 41 (2012): 363, https://doi.org/10.1007/s10508-011-9748-y.

41   Carballo-Dieguez, "Recalled Sexual Experiences," 363.

42   Carballo-Dieguez, "Recalled Sexual Experiences," 363.

43   SOGI123 and its related resources are copyrighted by the ARC foundation.

44   Scott Beddall, "Learning About Our Bodies," *BC Teachers' Federation*, 2016, https://www.bctf.ca/classroom-resources/details/learning-about-our-bodies. See also Nick Monroe, "Canadian Kindergartners Given Masturbation Homework Assignment," *The Post Millenial*, May 13, 2022, https://thepostmillennial.com/canadian-kindergartners-given-masturbation-homework-assignment.

45   See in particular the work by Pierre Barns. Drea Humphrey, "Father Exposes Child Grooming Books in Canadian Schools," *Rebelnews*, August 13, 2022, https://

The work of sexologists like James Cantor and Michael Seto have provided the "expert" basis for the acceptance of pedophiles, or increasingly in the language of the literature, "minor-attracted persons." They argue that based on the peer-reviewed evidence and research, pedophilia is an innate "orientation" just like being gay or lesbian, that it is highly resistant to change, and that the best we can do for pedophiles is to de-stigmatize their orientation and keep them "virtuous" and from actually abusing children.[46]

If one accepts, a priori, that sexual desires themselves are morally neutral (or to be celebrated), and those desires which are highly resistant to change constitute "orientations," then why shouldn't pedophilia be an accepted orientation? The Christian, of course, believes that man's desires may be severely compromised or aberrant,[47] that sexual desires ought not to form the basis of one's identity, and that Christ and the power of the Holy Spirit can change even the most resistant sinful desires. Other than cultural intuition, however, the secular world does not have the intellectual or moral resources to combat the twisted logic of this terrible trajectory. The full acceptance of pedophilia may not be far in the future.[48]

We are on the slippery slope down to Sodom. How long before an outcry against our sins reaches the ears of heaven (Gn 18:20) and the Lord rains down His judgment? Are we already experiencing that judgment?

---

www.rebelnews.com/father_exposes_child_grooming_books_in_canadian_schools.

46   For this reason, and in order to keep pedophiles from offending, Cantor is in favor of "treating" pedophilia with child-sex dolls and graphic depictions of adult-child sex, as long as no real children are incorporated or harmed. Benjamin Boyce, "A Crash Course in Sexology | with Dr. James Cantor," *YouTube*, 2019, https://www.youtube.com/watch?v=r6oJj6b5FQM; Michael C Seto, "Is Pedophilia a Sexual Orientation?," *Archives of Sexual Behaviour*, no. 41 (2012): 231–36, https://doi.org/10.1007/s10508-011-9882-6.

47   Of course, in an important sense, the doctrine of the depravity of man teaches that all of man's desires are aberrant when seen in the light of the holiness of God.

48   Just as the suicide of Josh/Leelah Alcorn propelled transgender issues into the public, all it may take would be one or two suicides of "gay" teens writing in their suicide notes that if the world accepted their relationship with their adult lovers, they would not have felt that they had to kill themselves.

SERVING SATAN

Alongside murder and sexual immorality, idolatry is featured as one of the great sins of Babylon and the Beast in the last days (Rv 13:15, 17:3, 18:6). Although the scriptures portray all pagans as false worshipers (Rom 1:23), and covetousness as idolatry (Eph 5:5), overt occultism and Satanism rise to the foreground in times of apocalypse. Nazi Germany is a salient example.

The Indiana Jones movies incorporate Nazi treasure hunters looking for powerful talismans and magical weapons. Similarly, in the opening scenes of Marvel's *Captain America: The First Avenger,* the Third Reich comic-book villain, The Red Skull, hunts for the otherworldly power of the "Tesseract." These fictional portrayals build on the historical reality of widespread occultism in Germany prior to, and during, the rise of its Nazi Antichrist, and a demonic obsession with mystical power. "In no country," asserts one witness, "were so many miracles performed, so many ghosts conjured, so many illnesses cured by magnetism, so many horoscopes read."[49] Although the Nazi party publicly opposed occultism, Nazi leaders were, antithetically, often private practitioners. They made significant use of "scientific" occult practices in research and even experimented with the development of "magical" weapons, like death rays and sound weapons.[50] Rudolph Hess, Deputy Führer until 1941, was a member of the Thule Society and a fervent occultist who practiced astrology and telepathy.[51] SS leader Heinrich Himmler funded occult-inspired endeavors like the search for the Holy Grail, had the prominent astrologer Wilhelm Wulff as his personal advisor, and collected a vast occult library of 13,000 books.[52] And then there is Hitler himself.

---

49   Erwin W. Lutzer, *Hitler's Cross* (Chicago: Moody Publishers, 1995), 84.

50   Eric Kurlander, "The Nazi Magicians' Controversy: Enlightenment, 'Border Science,' and Occultism in the Third Reich," *Central European History* 48, no. 4 (2015): 521, https://www.jstor.org/stable/43965203; Andrew Stuttaford, "Gods and Monsters," *The National Review,* 2017, https://www.nationalreview.com/magazine/2017/10/02/eric-kurlander-hitlers-monsters/.

51   Kurlander, "The Nazi Magicians' Controversy," 511; Lutzer, *Hitler's Cross,* 84.

52   Eric Kurlander, "Hitler's Supernatural Sciences: Astrology, Anthroposophy,

Erwin Lutzer chronicles Hitler's demonic influences in *Hitler's Cross*. These influences include forerunning occultists like Guido von List, Dietrich Eckart, and Houston Chamberlain, who pointed to their antichrist "messiah" in much the same way as John the Baptist announced the coming of Christ: "Hitler is an awakener of souls," heralded Chamberlain, "the vehicle of Messianic power."[53] But Hitler was also satanically inspired by his own studies of "yoga, hypnotism, astrology, and various forms of Eastern occultism."[54] The Führer's seemingly supernatural ability to hold sway with his hearers may very well have been demonic in origin. "Through rituals and pacts with demonic forces," Lutzer concludes, "he was changed into a man of such awesome power that skeptics regularly became fanatics just by listening to his speeches."[55]

The occult background of this recent antichrist movement is helpful in understanding how mysticism and even overt Satanism among political and cultural leaders can be easily overlooked, or treated as mere "play." Publicly, at least near the beginning of the Third Reich, Hitler and the Nazis represented themselves as Christians. Later on, as their masks came off, the German blood and race was elevated to the place of religion. Through it all, the German public remained mostly unaware of the demonism lurking behind their leaders. This should not surprise us, as Satan is a master of deceit, disguising himself as an "angel of light" (2 Cor 11:14.) As Satanist Aleister Crowley states in *The Book of the Law*, "Let my servants be few & secret: they shall rule the many & the known."[56]

There are signs currently that, just as in Hitler's day, major world figures are involved in mystical occult practices and even overt

---

and World Ice Theory in the Third Reich," in *Revisting the "Nazi Occult,"* ed. Eric Kurlander and Monica Black (Boydell & Brewer, 2021), 135; Ian Harvey, "Himmler's Witches Library Discovered in the Czech Republic," *War History Online*, 2016, https://www.warhistoryonline.com/featured/himmlers-witches-library-discovered-czech-republic.html?chrome=1.

53   Lutzer, *Hitler's Cross*, 74–84.

54   Lutzer, *Hitler's Cross*, 79.

55   Lutzer, *Hitler's Cross*, 83.

56   Aleister Crowley, *The Book of the Law*, Centennial (York Beach, ME: Red Wheel, 2004), 19.

Satanism. Marina Abramović is a Serbian performance artist whose "transgressive" art often features blood, nudity, and occult themes.[57] Abramović, whose Twitter handle is @AbramovicM666, has been featured in Vogue magazine holding goat's horns, and on a TEDtalk with a pentagram on her abdomen.[58] Even though she maintains she is not a Satanist, her occultism and mysticism are more than evident— "she goes in for shamanism, crystals, clairvoyants and star signs," one apologetic article states.[59]

Her 1996 performance "Spirit Cooking" is particularly shocking in its gruesomeness, and reveals the extent of her overt occultism. In it, Abramović uses pig's blood to write on a wall several occult "recipes," Satanic symbols including the pentagram and 666, and then splashes a small child-like statue with a pail full of the blood. "With a sharp knife cut deeply into the middle finger of the left hand. Eat the pain," reads one recipe scrawled in blood, "Mix fresh breast milk with fresh sperm milk. Drink on earthquake nights." (This little-known performance came under greater scrutiny in 2016 when in a leaked email from Abramović to John Podesta, Hilary Clinton's campaign manager, the occultist invited John and his millionaire brother Tony to a "Spirit Cooking" dinner at her place.)

Cannibalism seems to be a particular interest of Abramović. Several of her photoshoots and performative art events clearly feature the practice, some in which entertainers like Debbie Harry, Gwen Stefani, and Lady Gaga have symbolically participated.[60]

---

57   Ardjan Garcevic, "Understanding Marina Abramovic," *Balkan Insight*, 2017, https://balkaninsight.com/2017/03/29/understanding-marina-abramovic-03-15-2017/.

58   TED, "An Art Made of Trust, Vulnerability and Connection | Marina Abramović | TED Talks," *YouTube*, 2015, https://youtu.be/M4so_Z9a_u0; "Marina Abramovic & Crystal Renn for Vogue Ukraine August 2014," *A Stairway to Fashion*, 2014, https://astairwaytofashion.wordpress.com/2014/07/21/marina-abramovic-crystal-renn-for-vogue-ukraine-august-2014/. The Vogue photoshoot contains nudity.

59   Emine Saner, "Marina Abramović: 'I'm an Artist, Not a Satanist!'," *The Guardian*, October 7, 2020, https://www.theguardian.com/artanddesign/2020/oct/07/marina-abramovic-im-an-artist-not-a-satanist. Given her use of the goat's head, pentagram, and the number of the Beast in her "art," and other Satanist collaborators in her work, the claim to not be a Satanist is hard to believe.

60   Susan Michals, "Naked as They Came: Eating With Nudes at Marina Abramovic's LA MOCA Gala Performance," *Huffington Post*, November 14, 2011, https://www.huffpost.com/entry/naked-as-they-came-eating_b_1092843; "Marina Abramovic & Crystal Renn for Vogue Ukraine August 2014"; "Lady Gaga Artpops In at Watermill Benefit," WWD, 2013, https://wwd.com/eye/parties/gallery/lady-gaga-art-

Lady Gaga, one of the most successful pop superstars in history, has been particularly linked with Abramović. "I am obsessed with this woman," she said of the occultist performance artist in an interview.[61] In 2013, Gaga sought her out in order to learn her mystic methods. As part of her training "the singer didn't eat or speak for four days," relates *The Guardian*, "and found her way out of a wood, blindfolded and naked."[62] In support of her mentor, Lady Gaga released a bizarre and provocative video testimonial as part of a fundraiser for Abramović's Institute in which she appeared completely naked for much of it, including enveloping an enormous crystal with her body.[63] Abramović praised her young protégé for being determined and hardcore: "She never said it was too much, she said, 'I want more,' every time."[64]

Gaga's own songs and interviews suggest that the occult is not merely part of her renowned costuming. Several of her music videos are full of grotesque sex and occult imagery, and it is disturbing to think of the millions of young people who have been exposed to, and influenced by them. "Alejandro" is full of Nazi imagery, homoeroticism, and religious-occult visuals. In one scene, Gaga is surrounded by a gang of sinister, mostly naked men, and dressed in a white, latex nun costume, with a red inverted cross extending down to her genitals. "Judas" is another song rife with both Christian and anti-Christian imagery. It depicts a struggle between Jesus and the Judas in the entertainer's affections, once again with highly sexualized undertones and visuals. The song lyrics make clear who wins her love: "In the most Biblical sense, I am beyond repentance/ Fame, hooker, prostitute, wench vomits her mind/ But in the cultural sense, I just speak in future

pops-in-at-watermill-benefit/watermill-2013-lady-gaga-marina-abramovi263-robert-wilson-7069558-landscape/. Nudity is featured in some of these events.

61   Sleek Magazine, "Lady Gaga Speaks On the Impact of Marina Abramović," *Facebook*, 2020, https://www.facebook.com/sleekmag/videos/lady-gaga-speaks-on-the-impact-of-marina-abramović/1040686276309190/.

62   Saner, "Marina Abramović: 'I'm an Artist, Not a Satanist!'."

63   Billboard Staff, "Lady Gaga Strips Naked in NSFW Video For 'The Abramovic Method,'" *Billboard*, 2013, https://www.billboard.com/music/music-news/lady-gaga-strips-naked-in-nsfw-video-for-the-abramovic-method-5645258/.

64   Gil Kaufman, "Lady Gaga Is Marina Abramovic's 'Inspiration,'" *MTV*, 2013, https://www.mtv.com/news/loa8kd/lady-gaga-marina-abramovic.

tense/ Judas, kiss me, if offended, or wear ear condom next time/ I wanna love you/ But something's pulling me away from you/ Jesus is my virtue, and Judas is the demon I cling to."

In several of her interviews she has spoken of spirits influencing or oppressing her, including a frightening spirit named "Ryan" with whom she tried to communicate via séance with the help of a medium in 2010,[65] and a "devil force" inside of her who haunted her dreams in 2012.[66] In 2016 she named her album Joanne, after the entertainer's dead aunt, who she believes "installed her spirit in [her]," helping her to overcome a deadly cocaine habit early in her life.[67]

There are many other Hollywood stars known for their embrace of the occult,[68] but perhaps the entertainment industry's embrace of Satanism is most clearly seen in a recent animated series called *Little Demon*.[69] Disney, the parent company of FX Network, describes the show:

> Thirteen years after being impregnated by Satan, a reluctant

65   "Lady Gaga Haunted by Male Ghost," *NDTV*, 2012, https://www.ndtv.com/entertainment/lady-gaga-haunted-by-male-ghost-617219.

66   "Lady Gaga Haunted by Devil," *NDTV*, 2012, https://www.ndtv.com/entertainment/lady-gaga-haunted-by-devil-623576.

67   Thomas Smith, "Who Is The 'Joanne' That Inspired Lady Gaga's New Album Title?," *NME*, 2016, https://www.nme.com/blogs/nme-blogs/who-is-joanna-on-lady-gagas-album-1554917; "Lady Gaga Said Her Dead Auntie Joanne's Ghost Saved Her from Cocaine Addiction," News.com.au, 2010, https://www.news.com.au/entertainment/music/lady-gaga-said-her-dead-auntie-joannes-ghost-saved-her-from-cocaine-addction/news-story/4a32301958c893c586dc7c6a3f2e939a.

68   Megan Fox and Machine-Gun Kelly ritually drink each other's blood and there are strong suggestions that Travis Barker and Kourtney Kardashian do too. Lisa Respers France, "Megan Fox Has a Blood Drinking Ritual with Machine Gun Kelly and Thinks Social Media Is 'Sinister,'" *CNN Entertainment*, 2022, https://www.cnn.com/2022/04/27/entertainment/megan-fox-machine-gun-blood/index.html; Vigilant Citizen, "Megan Fox Openly Admits That She Drinks Blood For 'Ritual Purposes,'" *Vigilant Citizen*, 2022, https://vigilantcitizen.com/latestnews/meganfoxblood/. James Franco is an occultist who is associated with Abramovic and whose video for "Love in the Old Days" (for his band Daddy) features extensive nudity, and a Satanic-ritual wedding, presided over by Kenneth Anger, one of the most renowned Satanists of our generation. "James Franco's Satanic 'Love in the Old Days' Video," *Beginning and End*, 2013, https://beginningandend.com/james-francos-satanic-love-in-the-old-days-video/. For another example from the music business, see Vigilant Citizen, "Charli XCX and Her Story About Selling Her Soul for Fame," 2022, https://vigilantcitizen.com/musicbusiness/charli-xcx/.

69   All following details taken from "There's Something Wrong With Disney's 'Little Demon' and Its Executive Producer Dan Harmon," *Vigilant Citizen*, 2022, https://vigilantcitizen.com/latestnews/theres-something-wrong-with-disneys-little-demon-and-its-executive-producer-dan-harmon/.

mother, Laura, and her Antichrist daughter, Chrissy, attempt to live an ordinary life in Delaware, but are constantly thwarted by monstrous forces, including Satan, who yearns for custody of his daughter's soul.

The cartoon features Satanic ritualism, blood sacrifices, and a blasphemous "trinity" featuring an upside-down cross. The title screen for the show has in the background the sigil of Baphomet, with its goat's head within the pentagram. If this isn't chilling enough, the show's producer, Dan Harmon, is known for creating an abhorrent comedy short called *Daryl*, in which his character, a psychologist, rapes a baby, twice.

Slowly but surely, the most aberrant and malevolent practices are being normalized within our culture, and the fact that these despicable actions and productions do not result in ostracization from Hollywood, let alone arrests, suggests that just as in Hitler's day, occultism may be much more widespread than we know. Like the prophet Ezekiel, who in a vision was commanded to dig through a wall, and only then was shown the widespread abominations of Israel's leaders which they carried on in private (Ez 8:7–13), much of the abhorrent false worship of the world and its leaders may remain hidden for some time, but the Lord will reveal it all at some point.

In some cases, it may be that these leaders do not fully know what they are doing as they participate in demonically influenced activities. But in and of itself, the ignorance of those who participate in these practices is no hindrance to Satan using them, or gaining control over their lives and influence. In *The Last Battle*, C. S. Lewis illustrates this principle when a foul and fearful demon, the "god" Tash, comes to Narnia after he is summoned. Having just seen the foul creature, Jewel the Unicorn concludes, "It seems, then… that there is a real Tash, after all."[70]

"Yes," said the Dwarf. "And this fool of an Ape, who didn't believe in Tash, will get more than he bargained for! He called for Tash: Tash has come."

"Where has it—he—the Thing—gone to?" said Jill.

---

70   C. S. Lewis, *The Last Battle* (Harmondsworth, England: Puffin Books, 1978), 77.

"North into the heart of Narnia," said Tirian. "It has come to dwell among us. They have called it and it has come."

"Ho, ho, ho!" chuckled the Dwarf, rubbing its hairy hands together. "It will be a surprise for the Ape. People shouldn't call for demons unless they really mean what they say."[71]

Some of our world leaders and influencers may be ignorantly calling for demons, while others may be willful in their worship of Satan, but the results may not be much different. We have called for demons, and they have come.

Will those who name themselves Christian bow to the pressure of idolatry? Will the righteous be unequally yoked with the lawless (2 Cor 6:14)? Will we who were called into the fellowship of the Son (1 Cor 1:9), and feast regularly upon Him, share a table with demons (1 Cor 10:20–21)?

PROXIMITY AND PARTICIPATION

One of the most poignant images anywhere in Scripture is of a man washing his hands. He was a man of power and authority, but also a man under pressure. His wife had been warned by God in a dream (Mt 27:19) and his own sense of logic and justice led him to attempt an acquittal (Lk 23:4, 13–16), but at the end of the day, he bowed to the pressure upon him, and he allowed an innocent man to be murdered for crimes of which He was not guilty. To signal his lack of complicity in the matter of the man's execution, he washed his hands in water. The Jews may have been the ones who shouted, "let his blood be upon us and our children" (Mt 27:25), but that did not absolve Pilate of his sins. He was complicit, and for everything we know, he will forever be punished in hell for knowing what was right and failing to do it, which the scriptures call sin (Jas 4:17).

One day the judgment of God will fall, and we are warned to take no part in the sins of Babylon lest we share in her destruction (Rv

---

71   Lewis, *The Last Battle*, 77.

18:4). Sadly, many Christians have never seriously considered what constitutes complicity in sin.[72] We cannot register some small objection, turn a blind eye, and proclaim ourselves free of guilt: "we are innocent of this blood." It is God who judges. He will determine whether we have taken part in the world's evil or not.

A somewhat obscure passage from the Law gives considerable instruction and warning about complicity in serious moral evils. Deuteronomy 21:1–9 details the procedure for dealing with an unsolved murder outside of a city's wall. The distance to the murder scene was to be measured, and the elders of the closest city carried the responsibility for the ritual, which involved an atoning death. They were to take a heifer to a valley with running water and break its neck there. The priestly judges were to witness the sacrifice, the washing of the elders' hands, and their statement, "our hands did not shed this blood, nor did our eyes see it shed." Only in this way was the guilt of innocent blood purged from the people.

Innocence in the evil matter of the murder was only proclaimed because the elders had not *seen* the evil. It is presumed that if they had knowledge of the murder, the elders would have acted in using their authority to bring the perpetrator to justice—capital punishment in the case of murder. Although there is a special responsibility which the elders had here because of their authority, there is a connection between guilt and the knowledge of sin which undergirds many cases in Scripture. In the case of an ox who had gored a man to death, the ox was put to death, but the owner was not otherwise punished. However, if the ox was accustomed to gore in the past, and the owner

---

72   The issue of complicity in other's sins in ethics is, admittedly, complex. Not all proximity to sin is sin. The Lord Jesus provided wine to a wedding at which, it is safely presumed, some people became drunk (Jn 2:1–11). Christ was Himself called a drunkard for his regular association and fellowship with sinners (Mt 11:19). The "manualists" of the Roman Catholic tradition have done some helpful and excellent work on cooperation with sin and complicity. They have differentiated between "formal cooperation," in which one's will is aligned in a sinful act, and "moral cooperation," in which the cooperator does not will the sinful act. Formal cooperation is always sin, whereas moral cooperation is sometimes sin, as in the case of the father driving his daughter to the abortion clinic, and sometimes not, as with a mail carrier who delivers mail to an abortion clinic (which may contain helpful letters, documents, or payments) among his many other stops. See Germain Grisez, "Difficult Moral Questions. Appendix 2: Formal and Material Cooperation in Others' Wrongdoing," *The Way of the Lord Jesus*, n.d., http://www.twotlj.org/G-3-A-2.html.

did nothing about it, he too was to be put to death (Ex 21:28–29). Saul is portrayed prior to his conversion as a culpable accomplice in the stoning of Stephen. Although he had no authority as a "young man," he gave his assent to the murder as the keeper of the killers' garments (Acts 7:58).

The same principle underlies Paul's instructions about eating meat dedicated to idols. If a Christian was eating at an unbeliever's house, they were permitted to eat whatever meat was put in front of them, even if there was a possibility that it had been dedicated to an idol. But if the Christian was told that it had been offered in sacrifice then they were forbidden from partaking (1 Cor 10:27–28). The reason for guilt here is different than in the case of the unsolved murder but the guilt is still predicated on the knowledge of sin.[73]

The principle seen in these passages raises uncomfortable questions about Christian ethics in a world of increasing murder, sexual immorality, and idolatry. The pressures exerted by the Beast-system will increasingly tempt believers to subtly but seriously compromise by cooperating in the worst sorts of evils.[74]

The father who drives his teenage daughter to the abortion clinic thinking "she will do it anyway;" the son who holds his mother's hand while she undergoes a euthanasia procedure; the nurse who hands the needle to the doctor performing the act; they are all complicit in murder. The executive who calls himself an LGBT ally, the policeman who wears a rainbow patch on his uniform, the teacher who allows their students to be exposed to inappropriate sexual content at a school assembly; they are all complicit in sexual immorality.

---

73   In this case the issue is not the Christian's conscience, who has freedom to consider the idol as nothing, but the conscience of the pagan who views the silence and eating of the meat as sanctioning their idolatry. Leon Morris, *1 Corinthians: An Introduction and Commentary* (Downers Grove, IL: InterVarsity Press, 1985), 146.

74   It seems to me that the degree of evil ought to be considered in the matter of a response to sin and complicity. Murder, as the preeminent sin against man, is treated differently in Scripture than lesser sins, even compared to sins in the same category, such as anger. Murder, the spilling of blood upon the ground, cries out to God for justice in a way that is never predicated of anger (Gn 4:10, 2 Kgs 9:26, Is 26:21 Jas 5:4). We know intuitively that we are not responsible to intervene every time two people exchange angry words in public, but if we were to witness a knife attack, or an adult repeatedly striking a young child in the face, we would feel that something must be done.

Not every sin requires public protest. But every sin requires an abhorrence of it, and a distancing of ourselves from it in the fear of God and His judgment. "Save others by snatching them out of the fire; to others show mercy with fear, hating even the garment stained by the flesh" (Jude 23). The scriptures are clear that sin is not merely an act of commission, but may be an act of omission as well. "So whoever knows the right thing to do and fails to do it, for him it is sin" (Jas 4:17).

The German church's turning a blind eye to the Jewish holocaust is one of the clearest examples. "How could so many reputable and responsible churchmen have lent their support," asks historian J. S. Conway, "even if only passively, to the perpetration of such crimes as genocide?"[75] There was much that was hidden from the German public and the churches, but this hardly absolved the saints. As Pastor Maas of the Heidelberg Confessing Church responded, "Was not what we *did* see and hear quite enough?"[76] Erwin Lutzer provides an example in *When a Nation Forgets God*:

> A railroad track ran behind our small church and each Sunday morning we could hear the whistle in the distance and then the wheels coming over the tracks. We became disturbed when we heard the cries coming from the train as it passed by. We realized that it was carrying Jews like cattle in the cars! Week after week the whistle would blow. We dreaded to hear the sound of those wheels because we knew that we would hear the cries of the Jews en route to a death camp. Their screams tormented us. We knew the time the train was coming and when we heard the whistle blow we began singing hymns. By the time the train came past our church we were singing at the top of our voices. If we heard the screams, we sang more loudly and soon we heard them no more. Years have passed and no one talks about it anymore. But I still hear that train whistle in my sleep. God forgive me; forgive all of us who called ourselves Christians yet did nothing to intervene.[77]

"Rescue those who are being taken away to death," Proverbs

75   J. S. Conway, *The Nazi Persecution of the Churches 1933–1945* (Vancouver: Regent College Publishing, 1968), 331.

76   Conway, *The Nazi Persecution*, 332.

77   Erwin W. Lutzer, *When a Nation Forgets God*, Kindle (Chicago: Moody Publishers, 2010), 25–26.

24:11–12 directs, "hold back those who are stumbling to the slaughter. If you say, 'Behold, we did not know this,' does not he who weighs the heart perceive it? Does not he who keeps watch over your soul know it, and will he not repay man according to his work?'" As Paul warns Timothy, do not "take part in the sins of others; keep yourself pure" (1 Tm 5:22).

DRAW YOUR LINES IN ADVANCE

I was greatly benefitted by having faithful pastors growing up in a Baptist church. One of them, a preacher and strategist, a man of great piety and vision, discipled and challenged me, and especially through his preaching. I recall several of his sermons quite vividly. On one occasion he recounted an interaction with a self-confessing Christian in our town who had recently begun living with a woman other than his wife (without using the man's name). Above all else, he lamented the blot that this was to the glory of the Lord Jesus Christ. He stated that he had asked the Lord that if he were ever on his way to such a sin, that God would strike him dead rather than let him publicly denigrate His name. That made a great impression upon me as a young man.

Vows do not get much attention or use in modern evangelicalism. This is not altogether wrong. Both James and Jesus warn against using vows, as they can be used to undermine lives of simple truth and witness—better to simply say "yes" or "no" (Mt 5:37, Jas 5:12). In a broader view, however, vows, or more informal commitments like resolutions, have a very significant place in the faith of the saints in Scripture. In fact, Old Testament piety was often summed up in the idea of keeping one's vows (Ps 61:8, 65:1). A vow helped the Rechabites stay true to the Lord though centuries, as we have already considered, and the apostle Paul undertook vows several times (Acts 18:18, 23–24).

Vows, resolutions, and commitments can help the saint in bolstering a weak will. When these commitments are made in advance, they can provide the skeletal strength upon which the musculature of faith may be exercised on an occasion of struggle. The moment of pressure, when disapproval or loss looms large, is not the time for difficult decision-making. Moral decisions that may seem black and white to us now may not appear so years in the future as the darkness grows around us. We need to draw our lines in advance.

Resolve in advance that you will not ever be in the same room in which a person is committing suicide through euthanasia. Resolve in advance that you will not ever sign a "diversity" or "inclusion" agreement that the world would understand to be an assent to LGBT ideology. Resolve in advance that you will not accept a global biometric identification or put anything within your body that would permit anyone other than God to survey, control, or influence your decisions.

These determinations above, as best as I understand them, are black-and-white matters of Christian faithfulness. But this is not the beginning and end of our moral decision-making. There is also the matter of each individual's conscience. Like the issue of complicity and cooperation in other's sins, the issue of the conscience is poorly understood and almost as rarely preached upon in the church. This has been made exceptionally clear in the recent matter of vaccine mandates in churches and Christian organizations.

The decision-making process for many groups has been to start from the presumption that if they are to continue to operate, they must enforce vaccination among their staff or attendees. According to Scripture, however, the starting point of any decision-making process must be that the saint is willing to do anything, and suffer any consequence, rather than sin against God—*anything*. By operating from the wrong starting point, many groups sinned against their members, fellow-workers, and brothers, by pressuring them, contrary to their conscience, to be vaccinated.[78] That such constraints have been instituted by churches and seminaries seems to me to be nothing short

---

78   I am presenting the argument somewhat simply. There are organizations, especially where overseas travel is required, that demand certain vaccinations. The line may not be black and white. Nevertheless, it seems clear that the threshold for mandates in this case was not close to being met. Among the reasonable concerns of objectors were that the vaccines were experimental and not rigorously tested, that the new mRNA platform could react differently or have longer-term adverse effects, that they were unnecessary due to the mortality risk being very low except for the elderly or those with co-morbidities, or that they, as individuals, had immunity from prior infection. With what we have discovered since the vaccine rollouts, the mandates by churches and Christian organizations appear more unethical still.

of contemptible. These are places where the mutual confession of agreed-upon doctrine is the basis for fellowship, and where issues of conscience are not only to be respected, they ought to be determinative, lest a brother be caused to stumble. There is no lack of clarity on these matters in Scripture.

"Let us not pass judgment on one another any longer," teaches the apostle Paul, "but rather decide never to put a stumbling block or hindrance in the way of a brother" (Rom 14:13). We who are strong have an obligation to bear with the failings of the weak, and not to please ourselves" (Rom 15:1), he states a little later. It is through the extension of grace to the convictions of our brothers' consciences that we are to "live in such harmony with one another" that we may with "one voice glorify the God and Father of our Lord Jesus Christ" (Rom 15:5–6). "Therefore welcome one another as Christ has welcomed you," Paul concludes, "for the glory of God" (Rom 15:7). How can we possibly obey these commands if people have been excluded from fellowship, assembly, or co-labouring on account of holding fast to the convictions of their conscience?

Whether the issue is one of clear-cut Christian morality, or one of personal convictions led by your conscience, you must determine not to sin against God or others. Your commitment may mean the loss of relationships, the loss of a job, or even the loss of life. Draw your lines beforehand, so you are ready for that moment if and when it comes.

FUNERAL-LIVING

August Landmesser is a name I suspect few people know. And yet many people know his face. August was born in Germany in 1910, and in 1931, as a young man, he decided to join the Nazi party because he believed it would help him land a job in a very difficult economy.[79] Landmesser was never aligned with Nazi ideology, however, and in

---

79   "A Lone Man Refusing to Do the Nazi Salute, 1936," *Rare Historical Photos*, https://rarehistoricalphotos.com/august-landmesser-1936/. Everything subsequent about Landmesser is taken from this source.

1934 he fell in love with a Jewish woman by the name of Irma Echler. A year later he became engaged to Irma and was expelled from the party, with their application for marriage also being denied.

The famous picture of August Landmesser comes from the following year, 1936. At the launch of a German boat, there was a ceremony attended by Hitler himself. The black and white picture shows hundreds of men, young and old, soldiers and workmen, likely from a great variety of backgrounds and positions in German society. In spite of this diversity each one of them has their arms stretched out like an army phalanx towards their commander in a hail. All except for one man. Rather than having his arms raised, August has them folded across his chest with a defiant scowl on his face—a single dissenter in a sea of evil conformity.

Landmesser's story, including his wife's death at a Euthanasia Centre, his incarceration in a concentration camp, and his eventual death in 1943 as a penal conscript, reminds me of the biblical account of three young Hebrew men who refused to bow to an image of Nebuchadnezzar on the plains of Shinar. It was a circumstance that was designed to pressure the many dignitaries of the Babylonian empire to conform in deference and worship of this pagan king. Visually, there was the central image as the object of worship and the fiery furnace as a looming threat. Auditorily, there was the sound of "horn, pipe, lyre, trigon, harp, bagpipe, and every kind of music," which signalled the moment of compliance (Dn 3:5). In spite of the perfect orchestration of the production, three refused to bow—Shadrach, Meshach and Abednego.

Furious, Nebuchadnezzar demanded that they prostrate themselves in worship. If they did not, he threatened, "you shall immediately be cast in a burning fiery furnace. And who is the god who will deliver you out of my hands?" (Dn 3:15). The answer of the three Jews is interesting. They believed that God was capable of saving them with a mighty miracle— "our God whom we serve is able to deliver us from the burning fiery furnace, and he will deliver us out of your hand, O king" (Dn 3:17). But even if God chose not to save them, they theorized, they were willing not only to lose face in front of their peers and

to lose their well-paying government jobs, but to lose their very lives—
"But if not, be it known to you, O king, that we will not serve your
gods or worship the golden image that you have set up" (Dn 3:16–18).

The saint must be constantly ready to die: to the world, to self,
and in body. Following Christ is predicated upon this truth.

> If anyone would come after me, let him deny himself and take
> up his cross and follow me. For whoever would save his life will lose
> it, but whoever loses his life for my sake will find it. For what will it
> profit a man if he gains the whole world and forfeits his soul? Or what
> shall a man give in return for his soul? (Mt 16:24–26)

The Christian is to live dead. As Paul stated, "I die every day"
(1 Cor 15:31). This funeral-living is to characterize every minute of
the saint's life and it frees us to live without fear of loss or death. In
Christ, we have already died. To lose all things is to gain the riches of
heaven eternally. If instead we refuse to die at present, we will lose our
lives eternally. As C. S. Lewis writes, "Die before you die. There is no
chance after."[80] The only thing that comes after death is the assignment
to an eternal heaven or hell. In heaven, ultimately a renewed earth, the
saint will be welcomed to share the eternal joy of the Master he has
served faithfully (Mt 25:21). There will be never-ending pleasure in the
good God and all that He has created and redeemed through His Son
and Spirit.

In hell, the wicked who have refused to repent of their murders, sexual immorality, and idolatry (Rv 9:20–21) will share the
eternal punishment of everlasting fire with the demons and devils they
have followed (Mt 25:41). As the saint looks upon the villainy and
depravity of the world and its leaders, he may feel like "righteous Lot"
who was tortured in soul over the evils he saw in Sodom day after
day (2 Pt 2:7–8). But as Peter reminds us, "the Lord knows how to
rescue the godly from trials, and to keep the unrighteous under punishment until the day of judgment" (2 Pt 2:9). The time may be very
short. "Behold, I am coming soon, bringing my recompense with me,
to repay each one for what he has done" (Rv 22:12). Do not sup with

---

80   C. S. Lewis, *Til We Have Faces* (San Diego, CA: Harcourt Brace & Co.,
1984), 279.

Satan. Instead, eat and drink with the Lord of life. "The Spirit and the Bride say, 'Come.' And let the one who hears say, 'Come.' And let the one who is thirsty come; let the one who desires take the water of life without price" (Rv 22:17). Don't dine with demons.

Apocalypse-Preparation List

- Do not treat conspiracy theories as necessarily false. And above all, do not presume upon the good intentions of unbelievers—those the scriptures classify as "wicked."
- Resolve never to participate in the world's sins. Think seriously about what the scriptures teach about complicity in evil. Be willing to do anything, even to die, rather than to sin against God.
- Draw your lines advance. Before pressures mount, determine what you are willing or not willing to do.
- Listen to your own conscience, and protect the consciences of your brothers and sisters in Christ.
- Consider every moment of your life as lived in death to sin, self, and the world, so that you are ready, if necessary, to die bodily for Christ. Die now, because afterwards it will be too late.
- Memorize Philippians 3:7–11. "But whatever gain I had, I counted as loss for the sake of Christ. Indeed, I count everything as loss because of the surpassing worth of knowing Christ Jesus my Lord. For his sake I have suffered the loss of all things and count them as rubbish, in order that I may gain Christ and be found in him, not having a righteousness of my own that comes from the law, but that which comes through faith in Christ, the righteousness from God that depends on faith— that I may know him and the power of his resurrection, and may share his sufferings, becoming like him in his death, that by any means possible I may attain the resurrection from the dead."

CHAPTER 7

Find the Faithful

EVEN THE ELECT

On February 2nd, 2022, conservative journalist Megan Basham dropped a bombshell on mainstream "conservative" evangelicalism, and she had the audacity to name names. Writing for *The Daily Wire*, she accused Ed Stetzer, David French, Russell Moore, Rick Warren, and Tim Keller, among others, of having been church mouthpieces for Dr. Francis Collins and the National Institute of Health at the beginning of the COVID crisis.[1] "I want to exhort pastors once again to try to use your credibility with your flock," Collins stated on Ed Stetzer's podcast, "to put forward the public health measures that we know can work."[2]

At first glance, it may sound eminently reasonable for the government to enlist the help of church leaders to bring about a coordinated response to an international health crisis. And if so, Dr. Collins, a self-proclaimed evangelical Christian operating within the highest echelons of society and science, seems like exactly the right person for the job.

Basham's article, however, surfaces several problems. There is significant debate over multiple aspects of COVID, vaccines, masks, and lockdowns, and much more now than at the beginning of the COVID pandemic. Just how right or wrong was this "Christian ex-

---

1   Megan Basham, "How The Federal Government Used Evangelical Leaders To Spread Covid Propaganda To Churches," *DailyWire.Com*, February 2022, https://www.dailywire.com/news/how-the-federal-government-used-evangelical-leaders-to-spread-covid-propaganda-to-churches.

2   Basham, "How The Federal Government Used Evangelical Leaders."

pert" whom pastors not only trusted, but put before their people as an authority?

For example, Collins has vehemently argued against the Wuhan lab-leak theory.[3] However, major media outlets like the *Washington Post*, who once considered the idea "debunked" and a "conspiracy theory" are now seriously entertaining the likelihood of a leak.[4] There are several reasons for the narrative change. U.S. intelligence has emerged that "three researchers at the Wuhan virology lab had sought medical care in November 2019, a few weeks before officials disclosed the outbreak at the market."[5] Then there was the scandal surrounding *The Lancet*, one of the most reputable medical journals in the world, which in early 2020 published a statement that "roundly rejected the lab-leak hypothesis, effectively casting it as a xenophobic cousin to climate change denialism and antivaxxism."[6] But as Katherine Eban wrote in *Vanity Fair*, the statement was not only signed, but organized by EcoHealth Alliance President Peter Daszak who had "repackaged U.S. government grants and allocated them to facilities conducting gain-of-function research," including at the Wuhan Institute of Virology. His bias and financial interest should have precluded his involve-

3   Rod Dreher, "Evangelicals: Who Are The Good & The Bad?," *The American Conservative*, 2022, https://www.theamericanconservative.com/evangelicals-who-are-good-bad-francis-collins-david-brooks/. Collins has subsequently argued that he has never ruled out the lab-leak theory completely, but only adjunct theories, like the fact that it is a "bio-weapon." Readers ought to consider the leaked emails between Collins and Fauci before deciding whether Collins' statements are responsible distinctions or deceit. Caroline Downey, "Fauci and Collins Dismissed Prominent Scientists Who Endorsed Lab-Leak Theory, Emails Show," *National Review*, January 11, 2022, https://www.nationalreview.com/news/fauci-and-collins-dismissed-prominent-scientists-who-endorsed-lab-leak-theory-emails-show/.

4   Paul Farhi and Jeremy Barr, "The Media Called the 'Lab Leak' Story a 'Conspiracy Theory.' Now It's Prompted Corrections — and Serious New Reporting.," *Washington Post*, June 10, 2021, https://www.washingtonpost.com/lifestyle/media/the-media-called-the-lab-leak-story-a-conspiracy-theory-now-its-prompted-corrections--and-serious-new-reporting/2021/06/10/c93972e6-c7b2-11eb-a11b-6c6191ccd599_story.html. There are also reports of COVID infection prior to the Wuhan outbreak. See Antonella Amendola et al., "Molecular Evidence for SARS-CoV-2 in Samples Collected from Patients with Morbilliform Eruptions Since Late 2019 in Lombardy , Northern Italy," *Environmental Research* 215, no. P1 (2022): 113979, https://doi.org/10.1016/j.envres.2022.113979.

5   Farhi and Barr, "The Media Called the 'Lab Leak' Story a 'Conspiracy Theory.'"

6   Katherine Eban, "The Lab-Leak Theory: Inside the Fight to Uncover COVID-19's Origins," *Vanity Fair*, June 3, 2021, https://www.vanityfair.com/news/2021/06/the-lab-leak-theory-inside-the-fight-to-uncover-covid-19s-origins.

ment in the *Lancet* statement.

It is possible, of course, that Dr. Collins was simply wrong (although leaked emails are more suggestive of a cover-up.)[7] However, as noted in chapter three, we live in an environment of cancel culture and media-driven narratives. How many intelligent, informed Christians were demonized by their churches or pastors for believing a "conspiracy theory" that increasingly looks likely?

Discourse on vaccine effectiveness and safety has also significantly changed since the beginning of the pandemic. Time will tell how reliable the VAERS database is at reporting vaccine side-effects, and to what degree it underestimates total vaccine injuries.[8] But it was not long ago that reports of serious adverse reactions were treated with ridicule. How many Christians have been influenced or pressured into being vaccinated by their churches or pastors? Or suffered serious adverse effects afterwards? It is my personal view that pastors ought to avoid suggesting medical treatment. Nevertheless, if pastors do dispense health advice, they had better be right or their entire ministry threatens to be undermined.[9]

"FAITHFUL PRESENCE"?

But there is a far greater problem with the Collins-Evangelicalism connection than the possibility of government-fed, pastor-propagated medical misinformation. Dr. Collins, who had previously led the Human Genome Project and authored the New York Times bestseller,

---

7   Downey, "Fauci and Collins Dismissed Prominent Scientists"; Hans Mahncke, "Fauci Responsible for Suppression of COVID Lab-Leak Theory, Newly Revealed Emails Confirm," *Lifesite*, 2022, https://www.lifesitenews.com/news/fauci-responsible-for-suppression-of-covid-lab-leak-theory-newly-revealed-emails-confirm/?utm_source=twlsn.

8   "Adverse events from drugs and vaccines are common, but underreported. Although 25% of ambulatory patients experience an adverse drug event, less than 0.3% of all adverse drug events and 1-13% of serious events are reported to the Food and Drug Administration (FDA). Likewise, fewer than 1% of vaccine adverse events are reported." Ross Lazarus et al., "Electronic Support for Public Health–Vaccine Adverse Event Reporting System (ESP:VAERS)," *Federal Agency for Health Care Research*, 2010, https://digital.ahrq.gov/sites/default/files/docs/publication/r18hs017045-lazarus-final-report-2011.pdf.

9   The evidence level required for pastors to give medical advice is, and ought to be, far higher than for not giving medical advice.

The Language of God, was often lauded as a prime example of a less combative and strident approach to Christian witness and influence in a post-Christian culture.[10] However, as Carl Trueman writes, "Collins' 'faithful presence' at the National Institutes of Health does not seem to have gone beyond that of

faithfully turning up to work."[11] Indeed, he leaves behind a legacy of serious and shocking ethical compromises. On June 4, 2021, Dr. Collins penned a personal letter as head of the NIH in recognition of Pride Month, in which he stated,

> Each June, the National Institutes of Health joins the rest of the country in celebrating Pride Month and recognizing the struggles, stories, and victories of those who are lesbian, gay, bisexual, transgender, queer, intersex, and others under the sexual and gender minority (SGM) umbrella. I applaud the courage and resilience it takes for individuals to live openly and authentically, particularly considering the systemic challenges, discrimination, and even violence that those and other underrepresented groups face all too often. As a White cisgender and heterosexual man, I have not had the same experiences, but I am committed to listening, respecting, and supporting those individuals as an ally and advocate.[12]

It ought to be plain that no Christian with even a modicum of scriptural understanding could pen such a letter. But it gets worse. Under Collins' watch as head of the NIH, horrific and anti-human research has been funded by the organization. Justin Lee, writing in *First Things*, states that in May 2019, the NIH approved, under Collins, "a research grant requested by University of Pittsburgh scientists who desired to graft the scalps of aborted fetuses onto rats and mice."[13] The study was published in 2020 and features disturbing photographs "showing patches of soft, wispy baby hair growing amid coarse rodent

---

10   Trueman, "Decadence on Display."

11   Trueman "Decadence on Display."

12   Francis Collins, "From the NIH Director: NIH 2021 Pride Month," *National Institutes of Health: Office of Equity, Diversity, and Inclusion,* 2021, https://www.edi.nih.gov/blog/news/nih-director-nih-2021-pride-month.

13   Justin Lee, "The Cautionary Tale of Francis Collins," *First Things*, October 29, 2021, https://www.firstthings.com/web-exclusives/2021/10/the-cautionary-tale-of-francis-collins.

fur."[14]

Since Basham's article, and in spite of her repeated journalistic attempts to contact pastors who platformed and praised Collins and his "Christian expert" views, not a single evangelical leader named in the exposé has denounced Collins or walked back their support. Large swaths of evangelicals likely continue to think he is an upstanding Christian and a scientific expert given by God as a gift to the church to navigate challenging times. This level of church collusion with the government is terrifying—not only because it has the potential to undermine trust in pastors and Christian ministries who uncritically echo erroneous government views, but more seriously because it makes churches complicit in the evils of the world and its anti-Christ system.

If the "conservative" Christian can no longer look to church leaders like Keller, Moore, and Stetzer, where should they look? As a corrupt, intrusive, and increasingly global world system grows in its power and influence, how do we ensure that we are supported and encouraged in our Christian faith? Where do we look to find the *truly* faithful?

EVERYTHING IS POLITICAL

It is a widely recognized trend in evangelicalism that Christians are increasingly choosing their church based on political alignment.[15] I have heard many leaders recognize this emerging reality and lament it. The truth, however, is that in a day of increasing evils and Beast-system power, the gospel of Christ will be increasingly political and divisive culturally, just as it was in the days of the early church or in Nazi Germany. Faithful believers will need to consider the politics of their church and leaders, just as they did in prior days of tribulation. Consider the irony that Collins' quiet, supposedly non-political ap-

---

14   Lee; Y Agarwal, C Beatty, and S Ho, "Development of Humanized Mouse and Rat Models with Full-Thickness Human Skin and Autologous Immune Cells.," *Sci Rep* 10, no. 14598 (2020), https://doi.org/https://doi.org/10.1038/s41598-020-71548-z.

15   Dean Inserra, "Will People Leave Your Church Over Politics?," *Lifeway Research*, 2020, https://research.lifeway.com/2020/09/03/will-people-leave-your-church-over-american-politics/.

proach within influential circles of government and science did not reduce his politicism. It merely resulted in deep moral compromise in a church-government program. His example ought to serve as a warning for all Christians. You cannot escape the political.

"Christ is Lord," has always been a political statement. It is an exclusive claim of dominion over the entire earth and all its spheres, including the political. The Lord Jesus has been given all authority in heaven *and* on earth (Mt 28:18). He is the head over every rule, authority, power, and dominion (Eph 1:21). He is "the ruler of kings on earth" (Rv 1:5). Theologians, however, disagree on the practical implications of these statements.

There are two major competing theories in historical Protestant thought on the interaction of church and state: the Two Kingdoms view (2K), and the Neo-Calvinist or Transformationalist view.[16] In overly simplistic terms, they differ on the sort of dominion Christians ought to have in the world—is it predominantly a spiritual dominion, or are we to work to bring Christ's kingdom here in the material world?

The Two Kingdoms view, currently espoused and championed by David VanDrunen and Michael Horton, more greatly emphasizes the distinction between the sacred and the secular; Christ rules the redeemed church through Scripture, whereas God rules the created world through natural law, to which all people have access. In this view, each believer belongs to two kingdoms—the (common) kingdom of the world and the (spiritual) kingdom of Christ. Apologists for the 2K view frequently use illustrations from technical vocations to point out what they see as the absurdity of the Neo-Calvinist view: there is no uniquely "Christian" plumbing, bridge-building, or cooking,[17] and they point to the fact that Christ never advocated for, or aspired to, an

---

16   The Neo-Calvinist view is sometimes called the Kuyperian view after Abraham Kuyper. For the purposes of brevity, I am not interacting with pietism, reconstructionism, or a classical two-kingdoms view.

17   Boot suggests that what initially seems like a strong argument fades away when the theoretical comparison is not within Western culture, built upon Judeo-Christian values and thinking over millennia, but with pagan societies where the gospel has not yet made significant inroads. Boot, *The Mission of God*, 381–82. Ironically, it may be said that the Two Kingdoms view can only hope to proliferate in societies that have already substantially benefitted from Neo-Calvinistic views of transformation.

earthly kingdom.[18]

In contrast, the Neo-Calvinist view claims that all the world belongs presently to Christ, and that the Christian is called to bring the world into subjection to the Lord through the Spirit and the Word. This idea is echoed in Abraham Kuyper's famous statement, "There is not one square inch in the whole domain of our human existence over which Christ, who is sovereign over all, does not cry, 'Mine!'" Although most Neo-Calvinists uphold the idea of natural law, they view it as an insufficient means of properly ordering the world because of the darkening of man's heart and mind. And so we need God's Word in every sphere, not only in the church.

I believe that it is this latter view that is more in keeping with the Scripture's teaching, for several overarching reasons. Firstly, as we have already considered, the cultural mandate of Genesis 1:28 teaches that man is to have a comprehensive dominion over the entire earth. This first command is never rescinded. It is instead re-stated to Moses after the worldwide flood (Gn 9:1–3) and is largely consistent with the promises to Abraham and his offspring (Gn 12:1–3). The Great Commission ought to be understood as a gospel and church-focused reiteration of the same initial mandate of comprehensive dominion (Mt 28:18–20).

Secondly, when Beast-like systems have reared their ugly heads throughout history, viewpoints that have more strongly dichotomized the sacred and the secular have failed, and not only in preserving morality in culture, but also in preserving a faithful gospel witness. The experience of the evangelical church in Nazi Germany is a sober and salient example. Germany was a widely Christianized nation when Hitler rose to power in 1933. Many Christian leaders, including eventual heroes like Martin Niëmoller, supported Hitler for many years

---

18   For a very brief overview of VanDrunen's two-kingdoms view, see Matthew Barrett, "Review: Living in God's Two Kingdoms: A Biblical Vision for Christianity and Culture by David VanDrunen," *Journal of Theological Studies* 62, no. 2 (2011): 817–21; David VanDrunen, "The Two Kingdoms and the Social Order : Political and Legal Theory in Light of God's Covenant," *Journal of Markets & Morality* 14, no. 2 (2011): 445–62. Although I do not agree with VanDrunen's views of politics generally, his insights on justice and the *lex talionis* are excellent.

because of his strong leadership on national and economic issues.[19] As Hitler consolidated his dictatorship, however, it became clear to many of the faithful that Nazi intrusion into the gospel affairs of the church was against God and Scripture, and they banded together to form the "Confessing Church," which issued the Barmen Declaration in 1934.

Although this document is rightly extolled as an example of courage in a time of tribulation, many Christians remain unaware of the document's limits and that even the faithful, "confessing" church almost universally failed to speak prophetically against the Nazis' treatment of the Jews and the Holocaust within German society. As one scholar notes, "The witnesses were silent."[20] Within this gospel-saturated culture, the Christian leaders who remained faithful were shockingly few.

What accounts for the almost wholesale failure of Christian leadership in Nazi Germany? In his conclusion to *The Nazi Persecution of the Churches*, J. S. Conway provides four answers, the first of which was their

> ...ingrained tradition to pietism. The tendency of many Christians to limit their religious loyalties to the narrow goal of personal redemption has undoubtedly led to sincere and devout lives and has inspired the successive waves of missionary movements. But their failure to carry their Christian principles into political life has opened the way for a dangerous subjectivism, which drew from its Reformation background the belief that "politics do not concern the Church", and an almost Manichaean conviction that the affairs of political and social life are irredeemable. [21]

---

19   The protest of the Confessing Church, writes Conway, was against the "heresies of the 'German Christians' and "was completely dissociated from political circumstances. For instance, even in Niëmoller's church, while denunciations of Reich Bishop Muller was were made from the chancel steps, Nazi flags hung on the walls and the Hitler salute was given by the congregation." Conway, *The Nazi Persecution of the Churches 1933–1945*, 84–85.

20   Stephen R. Haynes and Lori Brandt Hale, *Bonhoeffer for Armchair Theologians*, 1st edition, Armchair Theologians Series (Louisville, KY: Westminster John Knox Press, 2009), 51.

21   Conway, *The Nazi Persecution of the Churches*, 334–35. Conway goes on to state that "the danger of such a retreat into the sacristy was recognized and deplored by the authors of the Barmen declaration: 'We reject the false doctrine, as though there were areas of our life in which we would not belong to Jesus Christ, but to other Lords—areas in which we would not need justification and sanctification through him'. This positive statement concerning the Declaration and the Confessing Church needs to be tempered by his more extensive commentary on the Barmen Declaration supplied

If past history is any indication, a Two Kingdoms or non-political approach to gospel engagement will fail in future days of tribulation. And not only will it fail in extending Christ's kingdom, it will also
fail to keep the church faithful to God. Theologian A. A. Hodge asserts,

> There can be no compromise. The King said, with regard to
> all descriptions of moral agents in all spheres of activity, "He that is
> not with me is against me." If the national life in general is organized
> upon non-Christian principles, the churches which are embraced with-
> in the universal assimilating power of that nation will not long be able
> to preserve their integrity.[22]

In prosperous or peaceful days, it may be possible for the
church to pretend that being non-political is the more faithful Christian
view. But in days of persecution, you will need to look for brothers
who are prophets, pastors who are willing to go to prison, and churches
who bear the suffering marks of their master. When that time comes,
you will want to belong to a church that will openly discuss the ways
the political Beast-system is marking the world, and will appropriately
warn the saints. In that day, the church that wants nothing to do with
politics, and only wants to preach the gospel, will fail in their duties.

NEW GOD; NEW RELIGION

One of the characteristics of the Beast's last-days dominion will be the
role of religion in supporting its nefarious plans. Jesus warned in Matthew 24 that this would be the case.[23] "And many false prophets will
arise and lead many astray. And because lawlessness will be increased,
the love of many will grow cold" (Mt 24:11–12). "For false christs and

---

earlier (p82–87): "It must be emphasized, however, that the Confessing Church did
not intend to use the Barmen Declaration as a programme of political protest. Neither
in 1934 nor at any time afterwards was it the aim of the Confessing Church to become
the spearhead of political opposition to the Nazis or the organizers of resistance to the
tyranny which was to engulf the whole country. Nor did they take a stand in the early
years against such crimes as the murders of 30 June 1934, the persecution of the Jews
or the erection of concentration camps" (p84).

22   A.A. Hodge, "The Law of the Kingdom," in *Evangelical Theology* (London,
Edinburgh, New York: T. Nelson and Sons, 1890), 283–84.

23   Prophetic themes are recapitulated throughout Scripture and history, and
there are probably fulfillments of these warnings at other times in history as well, such
as in 70 AD.

false prophets will arise and perform great signs and wonders, so as to lead astray, if possible, even the elect" (Mt 24:24).

The second beast in Revelation, the False Prophet, seems to be the ultimate fulfillment of these prophecies. We are told in Revelation 13 that he will make the entire earth worship the first beast (v12), perform miraculous signs (v13), and deceive the world such that they make an idolatrous image of the beast (v14). Moreover, he will give life to the idol, cause those who do not worship it to be killed (v15), and be the instrumental cause of the Beast's mark (v16).[24] Interestingly, this second beast is only mentioned once more (Rv 16:13) before the narrative of his final defeat in Revelation 19:19–20,[25] while the first beast remains constantly at the fore in these chapters.

This brief survey helps us to understand two ways in which religion and political power are connected in the Beast's kingdom. Firstly, (false) religion is subservient to political and military power. In fact, everything is subservient to it, for even the Prostitute and the kings of the earth, though they benefit for a time in the last days, will be ruined and forsaken in the singular exaltation of the Beast (Rv 17:13, 16), a dark mirror of the obedience all the earth owes to Christ (Phil 2:10–11). This truth is reflected historically in the Hitler oath which many in the German Confessing Church so ardently opposed. One Nazi newspaper described a public ceremony of oath-taking this way:

> Yesterday witnessed the profession of the religion of the Blood in it its imposing reality. Yesterday saw the triumphant and decisive beginning of our fight to make National Socialism the only racial religion of the German people. Whoever has sworn his oath of allegiance to Hitler has pledged himself unto death to this sublime idea. There is no more room for doubts and uncertainties, no room of retreat.[26]

---

24   Three of these aspects are repeated in Revelation 19:20, which seem to take a triadic or tri-perspectival form: firstly, the signs, which are outwardly oriented, secondly, the marking, which is inwardly oriented, and lastly, the worship of its image, which is upwardly oriented.

25   Arguably, this passage too is part of the narrative of his defeat.

26   Conway, *The Nazi Persecution of the Churches 1933–1945*, 146–47.

Here we see a clear example of false religion serving ultimate, Beast-like power, an example made all the more pointed by the fact that this Nazi religion did not overthrow, but incorporated most of the German churches.

It is uncommon that anti-Christ regimes specifically and explicitly call for Christians to denounce Christ, although it does happen. What is far more common, as in the days of the Early Church, is that martyrdom comes when Christians refuse to bow to a (deified) political power. With characteristic wit, G. K. Chesterton remarks of the early martyrs,

> Most of them did not die for refusing to worship Mercury or Venus, or fabulous figures who might be supposed not to exist; or others like Moloch or Priapus whom we might well hope do not exist. Most of them died for refusing to worship somebody who certainly did exist; and even somebody whom they were quite prepared to obey but not to worship. The typical martyrdom generally turned on the business of burning incense before the statue of Divus Augustus; the sacred image of the Emperor. He was not necessarily a demon to be destroyed; he was simply a despot who must not be turned into a deity.[27]

So firstly, Revelation 13 helps us to see how religion is made subordinate to politics in times of tribulation. Secondly, we see there the universality of a global political power (represented by the Beast) and the parallel global false religion (represented by the False Prophet). Of the several signs in Scripture of the end times, it is a global false religion that seems to be the least immediate at present. But even here, the foundations are being laid.

Joe Boot's 2016 work, *The Mission of God*, insightfully describes the new and emerging world religion which is the inevitable result of Christianity's retreat from the public sphere. As at Babel, modern man desires to reach up to the heavens and supplant God. In chapter five, *I Saw Satan Fall: Utopia, the Counterfeit Kingdom of God*, Boot traces the utopian impetus of modern humanism and how it functions as a religion. "The utopian devotee may not seem religious,"

---

27   Chesterton, "St. Thomas More," 507.

he states, "since he rarely mentions God, judgment, salvation, heaven or hell. But he constantly formulates new doctrine, ceremonies, and sacrifices."[28]

The utopian also formulates new "churches," ideological families which provide transcendent purpose in an agreed-upon orthodoxy. Legutko observes,

> Because egalitarianism weakens communities and thus deprives men of an identity-giving habitat, it creates a vacuum around them. Hence a desire exists for a new identity, this time modern and in line with the spirit of militant egalitarianism. The ideologies fulfil this role perfectly. They organize people's consciousness by providing them with the meaning of life, and individual and collective purpose, an inspiration for further endeavors, and a sense of belonging. With the emergence of ideology the problem of a lonely individual in an egalitarian society no longer exists: feminism makes all women sisters; all homosexuals become brothers in a struggle; all environmentalists become a part of an international green movement; all advocates of tolerance join the ranks of a universal antifascist crusade, and so on. Once a man joins an ideological group all becomes clear to him and everything falls into place; everything is either right or wrong, correct or incorrect. And this perception soon changes the man himself.[29]

Black Lives Matter and the LGBT movement are prime examples of these new religious units. Around the fringes, these groups may sometimes bump into one another, as when Radical Feminists rail against transgender advocates concerning the disappearance of single-sex spaces and the undermining of women's rights. But on the whole, they travel the same humanistic, utopian trajectory towards a global unity of so-called equity and justice, which is the very antithesis of the true equity and justice found in God.

Boot states, "Therefore, by eliminating differences (discrimination) in economic prosperity, knowledge, health, gender, moral values and more, all mankind will be humanized and socialized, united as one universal mind and entity and the unity of the godhead will be

---

28   Boot, *The Mission of God*, 160.

29   Legutko, *The Demon in Democracy*, 137.

achieved."[30] Just as the early church was considered by the Roman Empire to be atheists, "those who oppose this [religious] vision are to be condemned as heretics, disturbers of the peace and purveyors of the new atheism—belief in the God of the Bible."[31]

Churches corporately, and believers individually, must resist the urge to join these ideological movements. The pressures are great. The Christian may tire of the incessant tension between his beliefs and those of the world, and when some societal movement comes along that initially looks good, or uses language of justice or equity, he may feel that here there is finally something in which he can participate in brotherhood with his fellow man. And there may be aspects of these ideologies and movements that are worth considering and upholding. But precisely because they function as new religions, he must not identify with them.

One of the ways these movements function as a religion is the litmus-test of their "doctrines." If the Christian identifies with the group in some way, but does not adhere to their full and complete creed, he will be cast out and maligned by the group just as strongly as if he had opposed the entire ideology. For many, the pressure to be accepted will at that point be too strong. They will fail the test and compromise. In his 1944 lecture, "The Inner Ring," C. S. Lewis warned university students emerging from the aftermath of World War II against this tempting desire to be accepted and thought well of within the world—a passion "most skillful in making a man who is not yet a very bad man do very bad things."[32] Describing the process, he cautioned,

> And you will be drawn in, if you are drawn in, not by desire for gain or ease, but simply because at that moment, when the cup was so near your lips, you cannot bear to be thrust back again into the cold outer world. It would be so terrible to see the other man's face—that genial, confidential, delightfully sophisticated face—turn suddenly cold and contemptuous, to know that you had been tried for the Inner

---

30   Boot, *The Mission of God*, 168.

31   Boot, *The Mission of God*, 168.

32   C. S. Lewis, "The Inner Ring" (University of London: C.S. Lewis Society of California, 1944), https://www.lewissociety.org/innerring/.

Ring and rejected. And then, if you are drawn in, next week it will be something a little further from the rules, and next year something further still, but all in the jolliest, friendliest spirit. It may end in a crash, a scandal, and penal servitude; it may end in millions, a peerage and giving the prizes at your old school. But you will be a scoundrel.[33]

Churches must resist the temptation to seek acceptance within the world. Sadly, the economies and ecosystems of the modern evangelical church render her particularly susceptible to ideological and political pressure.

ECONOMIES OF FAITHFULNESS

The cult of prominence and personality in the evangelical church has created carnage in recent years. Ravi Zacharias, Bill Hybels, Mark Driscoll, James MacDonald, and C. J. Mahaney are just a few of the many eminent church leaders who led large churches and organizations over the past decades only to succumb to temptation or moral compromise. More recently, Ed Litton, president of the Southern Baptist Convention, the largest denomination in the world, has been embroiled in a serious plagiarism scandal.[34] Mega-churches and their pastors dominate the landscape and conversation of Western Christianity. We read their books, go to their conferences, and listen to their sermons. Although small churches are by no means immune to moral failure, large churches and their pastors face particular pressures from the world which will only increase if the Beast-system gains further power. The faithful Christian must look beyond the trappings of outer success and use scripturally accurate criteria when choosing a church.

Christ's messages to the seven churches in Revelation illustrate how different His standards may be from those of the world. The church in Smyrna was under great trial, and poor in the eyes of the world, but the Lord Jesus called them rich (Rv 2:9). The church of

---

33   Lewis, "The Inner Ring."

34   Leonardo Blair, "SBC Pres. Ed Litton Apologizes for Copying JD Greear Sermon Without Credit," *The Christian Post*, June 29, 2021, https://www.christianpost.com/news/sbc-pres-ed-litton-apologizes-for-jd-greear-sermon.html. In my opinion, the video comparison of both sermons in the article is damning.

Philadelphia had little power, but the Lord found them faithful in the midst of persecution and rewarded them for it (Rv 3:9–10). In contrast to these churches of little worldly significance, the Laodicean church was outwardly rich and prosperous, and yet Christ described them as "wretched, pitiable, poor, blind, and naked" (Rv 3:17). And the church of Sardis had a wonderful reputation for being "alive," but the Lord stated tersely that they were dead (Rv 3:1).

In times of tribulation one of the marks that sets apart faithful leadership is suffering, and the modern evangelical church, with its large buildings, big budgets, and board-style governance, is ill-equipped for it.[35] When choosing a church and leaders to follow, use the principle given in Scripture—whether they have the "scars" of suffering to demonstrate their loyalty to the one who died for them (2 Cor 11:23–30, Gal 3:17).

Most of the "imitate me" passages in the New Testament are specifically related to suffering for the gospel.

> And you became imitators of us and of the Lord, for you received the word in much affliction, with the joy of the Holy Spirit, so that you became an example to all the believers in Macedonia and in Achaia. (1 Thes 1:6–7)

> For you, brothers, became imitators of the churches of God in Christ Jesus that are in Judea. For you suffered the same things from your own countrymen as they did from the Jews. (1 Thes 2:14)

And when Paul defends his ministry and authority (for the sake of others) he speaks firstly of his sufferings: great endurance, afflictions, hardships, calamities, beatings, imprisonments, riots, labors, sleepless nights, and hunger (2 Cor 6:4–5).

In Nazi Germany, if you were a believer looking to find the faithful, you would have had to choose among the few who were willing to suffer, be imprisoned, or even die for the cause of Christ. Martin Niëmoller was in prison awaiting a Nazi trial, Conway recounts in *The*

---

35   While I believe that a shared eldership is the biblical model of church governance, my critique here is aimed not so much at the fact of board-governance models in churches, but at the attendant temptation to select church leaders on the basis of secular criteria, rather than the upside-down economics of Christ's kingdom, with its premium on suffering for Him.

DEEP DISCIPLESHIP FOR DARK DAYS

Nazi Persecution of the Churches, when "he was visited by the prison chaplain, who asked him in astonishment: 'But Brother! What brings *you* here? Why are you in prison?'" To this, Niëmoller answered, "And, Brother, why are you *not* in prison?"[36] The days may be coming soon when true believers ought to only attend churches led by pastors who have been jailed or otherwise suffered persecution for their faith.[37]

Will future tribulation, then, spell the end of large churches? Not necessarily. In fact, it may very well be the case that churches willing to draw hard lines in our culture, speak out prophetically, and suffer the consequences, will grow significantly. As Nancy Pearcey observes,

> It is a common assumption that, in order to survive, churches must accommodate to the age. But in fact, the opposite is true: in every historical period, the religious groups that grow most rapidly are those that set believers at odds with the surrounding culture. As a general principle, the higher a group's tension with mainstream society, the higher its growth rate.[38]

The coming cataclysm, however, may be the end of large churches *as we know them*—with their seeker-oriented services, careful cultural sensitivities, and big productions. If they do survive, it will be by drawing their lines in advance, and counting everything they have, including their buildings and reputations, as rubbish compared to the surpassing worth of obeying and suffering for Christ (Phil 3:7–11). Smaller, leaner, and more decentralized congregations are more likely to flourish as they pay the price and are rewarded with fruitfulness in tumultuous days. Established churches ought to create plans now to decentralize, move into homes, or go underground, ready to be implemented should the need arise.

Hilary of Poitiers, often called the "Athanasius of the West" for his courage and fight against Arianism in the 4th century, knew the cost of conviction, having been exiled for three years under Emperor Con-

---

36   Conway, *The Nazi Persecution of the Churches 1933–1945*, 332–333.

37   Several Canadian pastors have recently been jailed for continuing to minister and hold services during the COVID pandemic, while other churches have been fined.

38   Pearcey, *Total Truth*, 261.

tantius, from 356 to 359.[39] After his reinstatement, Hilary continued the battle against Arianism. Although by nature a gracious and congenial man, he warned and wrote against Auxentius, the Bishop of Milan, whom Hilary was convinced was a theologically dangerous leader even though Auxentius denied being an Arian.[40] One of Hilary's concerns was a pragmatism that was too willing to compromise theological convictions when faced with state pressures and the looming possibility of losing what belonged to congregations. He wrote to the churches,

> But one warning I give you: be on your guard against antichrist. A dangerous affection for walls has seized upon you; in a mistaken way you venerate the Church of God as if it must be seated under roofs and in buildings, and you connect with such things the idea of peace. But is there a doubt but that antichrist will take his seat in these? To my thinking, the mountains and the woods and lakes, the very prisons and chasms, are safer; for in such places men of old, either abiding by choice or detained by force, used to prophesy by the Spirit of God.[41]

ESCAPE TO THE HILLS?

Hilary of Poitiers' words beg the question—are there times in which the church should withdraw from an evil society? Are we to recognize God's judgment and "escape to the hills" as Lot was urged to do in escaping Sodom (Gn 19:17)? Are we to "flee to the mountains" as the saints were directed by Christ in His warning of the destruction of Jerusalem (Mt 24:16)? What does it look like to heed the general command to "come out of her, my people" (Rv 18:4) in a day and age in which an evil world system is increasing its control and lurching toward a universal technocracy?

Morally and spiritually, it means ensuring that our witness and worship are in keeping with the truths and holiness of Christ. As evil

---

39   John Gibson Cazenove, *St. Hilary of Piotiers and St. Martin of Tours* (London; New York: E. & J. B. Young & Co., 1883), 29.

40   E. W. Watson, "St. Hilary of Poitiers: Introduction," in *Nicene and Post-Nicene Fathers 2.9: St. Hilary of Poitiers, John of Damascus*, ed. Philip Schaff and Henry Wace (New York: Christian Literature Company, 1899), xlviii–liv.

41   Cited from Cazenove, *St. Hilary of Poitiers and St. Martin of Tours*, 172–73..

increases we will need to draw lines in advance and hold to them no matter the cost. But is there a case to be made for *physically* removing oneself from places of evil or judgment?

One factor in making this kind of difficult decision is whether or not the judgment of God is clearly imminent. Wisdom states that "the prudent sees danger and hides himself, but the simple go on and suffer for it" (Prv 22:3). In Noah's day, the word of the Lord was clear that a judgment over all the earth was coming, and the only way of deliverance was through the ark of God (Gn 6:13–14). In the plagues upon Egypt, as their destructiveness increased, God spoke in such a way that not only Israelites, but even many Egyptians, were able to escape the catastrophic results (Ex 9:20–21). Jesus gave His Judean countrymen two signs for when they were to flee to the mountains: the abomination of desolation (Mt 24:15–16) and the encircling of Jerusalem by armies (Lk 20). Both signs were clearly fulfilled in 70AD in the attack of the Roman general Titus upon Jerusalem and the destruction of the temple. It is a regular pattern in Scripture that although the saints must suffer many tribulations, God often provides a means of recognizing and escaping the worst judgments within the outpouring of His general wrath. If there were clear indications from God that judgment was to come upon a particular place at a particular time, we would indeed be wise to flee.

In spite of these clear examples earlier in Scripture, however, it seems noteworthy that there is no similar clarion call in the Epistles or Revelation. The emphasis seems to be, rather, upon endurance and willingness to suffer.[42]

> Do not fear what you are about to suffer. Behold, the devil is about to throw some of you into prison, that you may be tested, and for ten days you will have tribulation. Be faithful unto death, and I will give you the crown of life. (Rv 2:10)

> And they have conquered him by the blood of the Lamb and by the word of their testimony, for they loved not their lives even unto

---

42   It is doubtful that the protection of God's people described in Rv 12:6, 14 should be interpreted to mean physical protection in a secure physical location. See G. K. Beale and D. A. Carson, *Commentary on the the New Testament Use of the Old Testament* (Grand Rapids, MI: Baker Academic, 2007), 1124.

death. (Rv 12:11)

> If anyone is to be taken captive, to captivity he goes; if anyone is to be slain with the sword, with the sword must he be slain. Here is a call for the endurance and faith of the saints. (Rv 13:10)

Although there does not seem to be a biblical command to escape or flee in the apocalyptic future, it would seem to still lie within the purview of wisdom and conscience for each believer to do what seems best and to take into account a wide range of factors: the spiritual health and physical safety of their family; whether or not specific and singular acts of idolatry are calling out for God's wrath upon a particular place; and if there are signs that God's judgments have already started, such as extraordinary hurricanes, fires, or (especially) earthquakes which seem targeted (Rv 6:12, 8:5, 11:13, 19, 16:18).

Whether or not individuals or churches consider some plan of escape or retreat in the future, the Great Commission must never be abandoned—neither in proclamation nor in presence. Underground or remote locations, where they occur, must be used to strengthen the saints for their ongoing mission within the world, one way or another.

In 1935, Dietrich Bonhoeffer was chosen by the German Confessing Church to lead an underground seminary in Finkenwalde, Pomerania. The students there engaged in a rigorous communal program of Bible reading, meditation, prayer, and discipleship. In *Theologian of Resistance*, authors Christiane Tietz and Victoria Barnett note that Bonhoeffer was clear that the seminary's fellowship was not for its own sake, but that it was preparing the pastors for the church struggle.[43] "The goal," the dissident stated, "is not monastic isolation but rather the most intensive concentration for ministry to the world."[44]

There may be a place and time for a temporary withdrawal, but we were left here as witnesses in the world (Jn 17:18) and to be cities upon a hill to shine brightly in the darkness (Mt 5:15). These are posts we are not free to abandon.

---

43   Christiane Tietz and Victoria J. Barnett, *Theologian of Resistance: The Life and Thought of Dietrich Bonhoeffer* (Lanham, MD: Naitonal Book Network, 2016), 57.

44   Tietz and Barnett, *Theologian of Resistance,* 57–58.

THE TRIUMPH OF THE FAITHFUL

The pressures upon the church are significant and increasing. Whether
or not the emerging apocalyptic trajectories result in the return of the
Lord in the near future, or in some future renewal as God gives man
more time, Christ promises He will build His church and that the gates
of hell will not prevail against it (Mt 16:18–19). Whether the saints are
enjoying the favour of society or are undergoing severe persecution,
the promises of Scripture do not change. We are to trust that God has
given us the land (Jo 1:3) and that He will never leave us or forsake us
in our calling to build the Kingdom of Christ (Jo 1:9).[45]

The saint can run against a troop, and leap over a wall. The
God who equips him with strength makes his feet like that of a deer
and sets him secure upon the heights. The Lord trains his hands for
war, so that he may bend a bow of bronze. To him has been given the
shield of salvation, with God's right hand supporting him. The saint
pursues his enemies and overtakes them. He does not turn back until
they are consumed. He thrusts them through so they are unable to rise.
The Lord equips him with strength for the battle and all those who rise
against the saint sink underneath him (Ps 18:29–39).

If this sounds too triumphalist or militaristic, consider that
these sorts of passages in Scripture rarely arise out of a context of
power, but more often out of persecution. The greater the subjugation
of the saint or assembly, the stronger are the promises of victory which
are given to them. To the embattled church at Philadelphia, the Lord
Jesus assured,

> I know your works. Behold, I have set before you an open
> door, which no one is able to shut. I know that you have but little
> power, and yet you have kept my word and have not denied my name.
> Behold, I will make those of the synagogue of Satan who say that they
> are Jews and are not, but lie—behold, I will make them come and bow
> down before your feet, and they will learn that I have loved you. (Rv
> 3:8–9)

---

45   The land-dominion promise in Joshua 1 is founded on the dominion mandate of Gn 1:28, but also strongly prefigures the Great Commission in Mt 28:18–19.

The storm clouds are gathering upon the horizon. They threaten darkness and a deluge in the coming days. Not every assembly will weather the storm, but as sobering as this truth is, the approaching upheaval will sift and strengthen Christ's people. The saints may be exiled or executed, impoverished or imprisoned, castigated or condemned, blacklisted or betrayed. The church will, nevertheless, conquer. As you face demonic deceit, political pressure, and even friendly fire, ensure that you have the right people around you to help you navigate the perilous waters of our increasingly wicked world. Find the faithful.

Apocalypse-Preparation List

- Beware of churches and organizations that have colluded with the government.
- Find a church that is willing to apply the gospel to all of life, including culture and politics, and where political conversation is not quashed.
- Look for pastors and elders that have a track record of suffering for the gospel, and imitate them in their suffering.
- Encourage your church to have a decentralization plan ready for times of tribulation.
- Do not join or identify with the new religions or ideologies: BLM, LGBT, etc.
- Reject isolationist or retreatist thinking. Trust that Christ will build His church and that it will triumph.
- Memorize Revelation 3:7–13. "And to the angel of the church in Philadelphia write: 'The words of the holy one, the true one, who has the key of David, who opens and no one will shut, who shuts and no one opens. I know your works. Behold, I have set before you an open door, which no one is able to shut. I know that you have but little power, and yet you have kept my word and have not denied my name. Behold, I will make those of the synagogue of Satan who say that they are Jews and are not, but lie—behold, I will make them come and bow down before your feet, and they will learn that I have loved you. Because you have kept my word about patient endurance, I will keep you from the hour of trial that is coming on the whole world, to try those who dwell on the earth. I am coming soon. Hold fast what you have, so that no one may seize your crown. The one who conquers, I will make him a pillar in the temple of my God. Never shall he go out of it, and I will write on him the name of my God, and the name of the city of my God, the new Jerusalem, which comes down from my God out of heaven, and my own new name. He who has an ear, let him hear what the Spirit says to the churches.'"

Printed in the USA
CPSIA information can be obtained
at www.ICGtesting.com
JSHW020215041223
52992JS00003B/8